ELTON JOHI
THE ILLUSTI
Compiled by Alan F

CU00792732

Omnibus Press
London/New York/Sydney/Cologne

This book © Copyright 1981 Omnibus Press
(A division of Book Sales Limited)

Exclusive distributors:
Book Sales Limited, 78 Newman Street,
London W1P 3LA.
Quick Fox, N.Y. 10023, USA.
Book Sales Pty. Limited, 27 Clarendon Street,
Artarmon, Sydney, NSW 2064, Australia.
Music Sales GmbH, Kolner Strasse 199,
D-5000 Cologne 90, West Germany.

Book design: Howard Brown
Photo research: Alan Finch

Introduction © Copyright 1981 Alan Finch

ISBN 0.86001.926.8
UK Order No. OP 41227

Typeset by DahDah Limited, London
Printed in England by
J.B. Offset Printers (Marks Tey) Limited

Page 4,5 Alan Finch Page 6,7 Bluesology Photographer
unknown Page 10 Rocket DJM Page 12 Rocket DJM Page
25 Rocket DJM Page 28 Chalkie Davis Page 36 Rocket
DJM Page 42,43 Rocket DJM Page 46 Rocket DJM Page
50,51 LFI/Rocket DJM Page 60,61 Rocket DJM Page 68,69
Rocket DJM Page 71 Rocket DJM Page 82 Brian Adis
Page 93 Rocket DJM

UK SINGLES
Page 5

UK/USA ALBUMS
Page 25

US SINGLES
Page 61

BOOTLEGS
Page 71

INDEX OF SONGS
Page 94

This is a discography of all officially released records by Elton John in the UK and the USA, excluding promotional, juke box, guest appearances as producer, and cover versions. The author is aware of such releases but they are too numerous to mention in this edition.

Included in this discography are all known unofficially released bootleg records featuring Elton John. Also included are the three records issued by 'Bluesology', Elton's first professional group.

Entries give details of original catalogue numbers, musicians, recording dates, studios, release dates etc. etc.

An index of the songs featured in this discography can be found at the end of this book.

Thanks to Rocket Records and Dick James Music for permitting the reproduction of their record sleeves and use of photographs.

Thanks to Ginny O'Sullivan and Laura Beggs, to Jill for putting up with endless records lying around. And, of course, thanks to Elton John for his music.

UK SINGLES

BLUESOLOGY – SINGLES

1 **COME BACK BABY** *Reg Dwight 2:42 (A)*
TIMES GETTING TOUGHER THAN TOUGH
J. Witherspoon 2:15 (B)
Fontana TF 594 (UK). Released July 1965
Producer: Jack Baverstock. Engineer: David Voyde.
Tape Operator: Roger Wake.
Studio: Philips Studios, London
Recorded: June 3rd 1965

2 **MR FRANTIC** *Reg Dwight 2:23 (A)*
EVERY DAY (I HAVE THE BLUES) *Chatman 2:30*
Fontana TF 668 (UK). Released February 1966
Producer: Jack Baverstock. Engineer: David Voyde
Studio: Philips Studios, London
Recorded: November 18 1965

3 **SINCE I FOUND YOU BABY** *Byrne/Lynch 2:47 (A)*
JUST A LITTLE BIT *Shuman/Lynch 2:33 (B)*
Polydor 56195 (UK). Released October 5, 1967
Producer: Kenny Lynch
Studio: IBC Studios, Portland Place, London
Recorded: August 1967

4 **I'VE BEEN LOVING YOU** *John 2:47 (A)*
HERE'S TO THE NEXT TIME *John 2:52 (B)*
Philips BF 1643 (UK) Mono. Released March 1, 1968
Producer: Caleb Quaye
Studio: Dick James Studios, London
Recorded: December 1967/January 1968

5 **LADY SAMANTHA** *John/Taupin 3:03 (A)*
ALL ACROSS THE HAVENS *John/Taupin 3:50 (B)*
Philips BF 1739 (UK). Released January 17, 1969
Producer: Steve Brown
Studio: Dick James Studios, London
Recorded: December 1968

6 **IT'S ME THAT YOU NEED** *John/Taupin 4:04 (A)*
JUST LIKE STRANGE RAIN *John/Taupin 3:43 (B)*
DJM DJS 205 (UK). Released May 16, 1969

Producer: Steve Brown
Studio: Olympic Studios, London *(A)* Dick James
Studios, London *(B)* Recorded: April 1969

7 **BORDER SONG** *John/Taupin 3:20 (A)**
BAD SIDE OF THE MOON *John/Taupin 3:11 (B)*
DJM DJS 217 (UK). Released March 20, 1970
Producer: Gus Dudgeon
Studio: Trident Studios, London
Recorded: January 1970
*"Border Song" features "The Barbara Moore
Choir", which appeared on the "Warm Summer
Rain" track, B Side of "Denver To LA".

8 **ROCK AND ROLL MADONNA** *John/Taupin 4:15 (A)*
GREY SEAL *John/Taupin 4:00 (B)*
DJM DJS 222 (UK). Released June 19, 1970
Producer: Gus Dudgeon
Studio: Trident Studios, London
Recorded: January 1970

9 **YOUR SONG** *John/Taupin 3.:57 (A)*
INTO THE OLD MAN'S SHOES *John/Taupin 3:59 (B)*
DJM DJS 233 (UK). Released January 7, 1971
Producer: Gus Dudgeon
Studio: Trident Studios, London
Recorded: January 1970

10 **FRIENDS** *John/Taupin 2:22 (A)*
HONEY ROLL *John/Taupin 2:57 (B)*
DJM DJS 244 (UK). Released April 23, 1971
Producer: Gus Dudgeon
Studio: Trident Studios, London
Recorded: October 1970

11 **ROCKET MAN** *John/Taupin 4:35 (A)*
HOLIDAY INN *John/Taupin 4:22 (B)*
GOODBYE *John/Taupin 1:45 (C)*
DJM DJX 501 (UK). Released April 1972
Producer: Gus Dudgeon *(A) (B)*

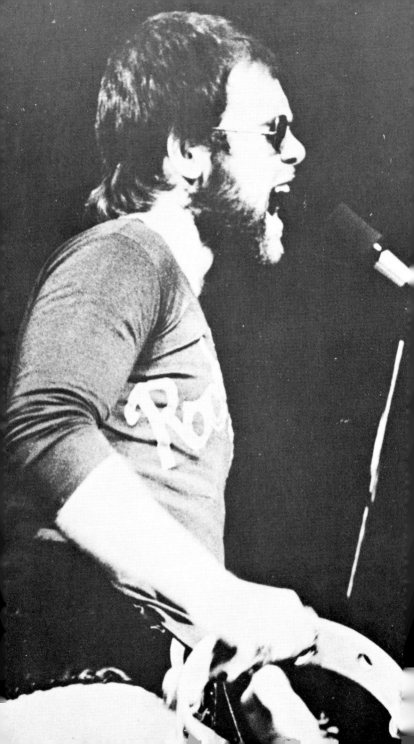

Studio: Strawberry Studios, Château D'Hierouville, France *(A)* Trident Studios, London *(B) (C)*
Recorded: January 1972 *(A)* August 9, 1971 *(B)*
February 27, 1971 *(C)*

12 **HONKY CAT** *John/Taupin 5:12 (A)*
LADY SAMANTHA *John/Taupin 3:03 (B)*
IT'S ME THAT YOU NEED *John/Taupin 4:07 (C)*
DJM DJS 269 (UK). Released August 1972
Producer: Gus Dudgeon *(A)* Steve Brown *(B,C)*
Studio: Strawberry Studios, Château D'Hierouville,
France *(A)* Dick James Studios, London *(B)* Olympic
Studios, London *(C)*
Recorded: January 1972 *(A)* December 1969 *(B)*
April 10, 1969 *(C)*

13 **CROCODILE ROCK** *John/Taupin 3:56 (A)*
ELDERBERRY WINE *John/Taupin 3:34 (B)*
DJM DJS 271 (UK). Released October 27, 1972
Producer: Gus Dudgeon
Studio: Strawberry Studios, Château
D'Hierouville, France
Recorded: June 1972

14 **DANIEL** *John/Taupin 3:52 (A)*
SKYLINE PIGEON *John/Taupin 3:45 (B)**
DJM DJS 275 (UK). Released January 1973
Producer: Gus Dudgeon
Studio: Strawberry Studios, Château D'Hierouville,
France
Recorded: June 1972
*This is a new recording
featuring piano instead of harpsichord.

15 **SATURDAY NIGHT'S ALRIGHT FOR FIGHTING**
John/Taupin 4:55 (A)
JACK RABBIT *John/Taupin 1:50 (B)*
**WHENEVER YOU'RE READY (WE'LL GO
STEADY AGAIN)** *John/Taupin 2:50 (C)*
DJM DJX 502 (UK). Released June 29, 1973

Producer: Gus Dudgeon
Studio: Strawberry Studios, Château
D'Hierouville, France
Recorded: May 1973

16 **GOODBYE YELLOW BRICK ROAD**
John/Taupin 3:13 (A)
SCREW YOU *John/Taupin 4:41 (B)*
DJM DJS 285 (UK). Released September 7, 1973
Producer: Gus Dudgeon
Studio: Strawberry Studios, Château
D'Hierouville, France
Recorded: May 1973

17 **STEP INTO CHRISTMAS** *John/Taupin 4:30 (A)*
**HO! HO! HO! WHO'D BE A TURKEY AT
CHRISTMAS** *John/Taupin 4:04 (B)*
DJM DJS 290 (UK). Released November 26, 1973
Producer: Gus Dudgeon
Studio: Trident Studios, London
Recorded: November 1973

18 **CANDLE IN THE WIND** *John/Taupin 3:50 (A)*
BENNIE & THE JETS *John/Taupin 5:10 (B)*
DJM DJS 297 (UK). Released February 1974
Producer: Gus Dudgeon
Studio: Strawberry Studios, Château
D'Hierouville, France
Recorded: May 1973

19 **DON'T LET THE SUN GO DOWN ON ME**
John/Taupin 5:33 (A)
SICK CITY *John/Taupin 5:22 (B)*
DJM DJS 302 (UK). Released May 1974
Producer: Gus Dudgeon
Studio: Caribou Ranch, Colorado USA
Recorded: January 1974 *(A)* April 1974 *(B)*

20 **THE BITCH IS BACK** *John/Taupin 3:40 (A)*
COLD HIGHWAY *John/Taupin 3:20 (B)*
DJM DJS 322 (UK). Released August 30, 1974
Producer: Gus Dudgeon
Studio: Caribou Ranch, Colorado USA
Recorded: January 1974

21 **LUCY IN THE SKY WITH DIAMONDS**
Lennon/McCartney 5:58 (A)
ONE DAY AT A TIME *Lennon 3:47 (B)*
DJM DJS 340 (UK). Released November 15, 1974
Producer: Gus Dudgeon
Studio: Caribou Ranch, Colorado USA
Recorded: July 1974

John Lennon Appears on
"Lucy In The Sky With Diamonds"
as Doctor Winston O'Boogie & His
Reggae Guitars

22 **PHILADELPHIA FREEDOM** *John/Taupin 5:38 (A)*
   I SAW HER STANDING THERE
   Lennon/McCartney 3:53 (B)
   DJM DJS 354 (UK) Released February 28, 1975
   Producer: Gus Dudgeon
   Studio: Caribou Ranch, Colorado, USA, *(A)* Madison
   Square Garden, New York City, (Live) *(B)*
   Recorded: June/July 1974 *(A)* Recorded Live
   November 28, 1974 featuring John Lennon *(B)*.

23 **SOMEONE SAVED MY LIFE TONIGHT**
   John/Taupin 6:45 (A)
   HOUSE OF CARDS *John/Taupin 3:09 (B)*
   DJM DJS 385 (UK). Released May 1975
   Producer: Gus Dudgeon
   Studio: Caribou Ranch, Colorado, USA
   Recorded: June 1974

24 **ISLAND GIRL** *John/Taupin 3:46 (A)*
   SUGAR ON THE FLOOR *Kiki Dee 4:31 (B)*
   DJM DJS 610 (UK). Released September 19, 1975
   Producer: Gus Dudgeon
   Studio: Caribou Ranch, Colorado, USA
   Recorded: June/July 1975

25 **GROW SOME FUNK OF YOUR OWN**
John/Taupin/Johnstone 4:45 (A)
**I FEEL LIKE A BULLET (IN THE GUN OF
ROBERT FORD)** *John/Taupin 5:30 (B)*
DJM DJS 629 (UK). Released January 9, 1976
Producer: Gus Dudgeon
Studio: Caribou Ranch, Colorado, USA
Recorded: June/July 1975

26 **PINBALL WIZARD** *Townshend 5:14 (A)*
HARMONY *John/Taupin 2:50 (B)*
DJM DJS 652 (UK). Released March 12, 1976
Producer: Gus Dudgeon
Studio: Ramport Studios, London *(A)* Strawberry
Studios, Château D'Hierouville, France *(B)*
Recorded: April 1974 *(A)* May 1973 *(B)*

27 **DON'T GO BREAKING MY HEART**
*Orson/Blanche 4:23 (A)**
SNOW QUEEN *John/Taupin/Johnstone/Dee/Nutter 5:54 (B)*
Rocket ROKN 512 (UK). Released June 21, 1976
Producer: Gus Dudgeon
Studio: Eastern Sound, Toronto
Recorded: March 1976
*Duet with Kiki Dee

28 **BENNY & THE JETS** *John/Taupin 4:15 (A)*
ROCK & ROLL MADONNA *John/Taupin 5:10 (B)*
DJM DJS 10705 (UK). Released September 9, 1976
Producer: Gus Dudgeon
Studio: Strawberry Studios, Château D'Hierouville,
France *(A)* Trident Studios, London *(B)*
Recorded: May 1973 *(A)* January 1970 *(B)*

29 **SORRY SEEMS TO BE THE HARDEST WORD**
John/Taupin 3:48 (A)
SHOULDER HOLSTER *John/Taupin 5:05 (B)*
Rocket ROKN 517 (UK). Released October 10, 1976
Producer: Gus Dudgeon
Studio: Eastern Sound, Toronto
Recorded: March 1976

30 **CRAZY WATER** *John/Taupin 5:40 (A)*
CHAMELEON *John/Taupin 5:25 (B)*
Rocket ROKN 521 (UK). Released February 4, 1977
Producer: Gus Dudgeon
Studio: Eastern Sound, Toronto
Recorded: March 1976

31 **THE GOALDIGGER SONG** *2:48 (A)*
JIMMY, BRIAN, ELTON, ERIC *11:50 (B)* *
Rocket GOALD 1 (UK).
Released April 1977
Producer: Elton John *(A)*
Recorded: March 1977
*Features Elton, Jimmy Hill, Brian Moore,
Eric Morecambe. Only 500 pressed for the
GOALDIGGERS' CHARITY for football.

32 **YOUR SONG** *John/Taupin 3:57 (A)*
ROCKET MAN *John/Taupin 4:25 (B)*
**SATURDAY NIGHT'S ALRIGHT FOR
FIGHTING** *John/Taupin 4:55 (C)*
**WHENEVER YOU'RE READY WE'LL GO
STEADY AGAIN** *John/Taupin 2:50 (D)*
DJM DJR 18001 (UK). Released May 17, 1977
Producer: Gus Dudgeon
Studio: Trident Studios, London *(A)* Strawberry
Studios, Château D'Hierouville, France *(B,C,D)*
Recorded: January 21, 1970 *(A)* January 1972 *(B)*
May 1973 *(C,D) Title of EP "4 From 4 Eyes"*

33 **BITE YOUR LIP (GET UP & DANCE)**
John/Taupin 6:50 (A)
CHICAGO *Conrad/Goodman 4:18 (B)* *
Rocket ROKN 526 (UK) 7" Version
Released June 3, 1977
Producer: Gus Dudgeon *(A)* Elton John/
Clive Franks *(B)*
Studio: Eastern Sound, Toronto
Recorded: March 1976 *(A)* September 1976 *(B)*
*By Kiki Dee

34 BITE YOUR LIP (GET UP & DANCE)
John/Taupin 6:45 (A)
CHICAGO *Conrad/Goodman 4:18 (B)**

Rocket RU 1 **(UK)** 12″ Version.
Released June 3, 1977
Producer: Gus Dudgeon *(A)* Elton John/
Clive Franks *(B)*
Studio: Eastern Sound, Toronto *(A)* The Manor,
Oxford *(B)*
Recorded: March 1976 *(A)* September 1976 *(B)*
*By Kiki Dee

35 EGO *John/Taupin 3:57 (A)*
FLINTSTONE BOY *John 4:07 (B)*
Rocket ROKN 538 (UK). Released March 21, 1978
Producer: Elton John/Clive Franks
Studio: The Mill at Cookham, Berks
Recorded: February/March 1978

36 FUNERAL FOR A FRIEND *John/Taupin (A)*
LOVE LIES BLEEDING *John/Taupin 11:05 (B)*
WE ALL FALL IN LOVE SOMETIMES
John/Taupin 4:15 (C)
CURTAINS *John/Taupin 6:12 (D)*
DJM DJT 15000 (UK) 12″ Version only.
Released September 16, 1978
Producer: Gus Dudgeon

Studio: Strawberry Studios, Château D'Hierouville,
France *(A,B)* Caribou Ranch, Colorado, USA *(C,D)*
Recorded: May 1973 *(A,B)* June 1974 *(C,D)*

37 **LADY SAMANTHA** *John/Taupin 3:03 (A)*
   SKYLINE PIGEON *John/Taupin3:30 (B)*
   DJM DJS 10901 (UK). Released September 18, 1978
   Producer: Steve Brown
   Studio: Dick James Studios, London
   Recorded: December 1968
   Entries 37 to 48 were available in a special box set.

38 **YOUR SONG** *John/Taupin 3:20 (A)*
   BORDER SONG *John/Taupin 3:57 (B)*
   DJM DJS 10902 (UK). Released September 18, 1978
   Producer: Gus Dudgeon
   Studio: Trident Studios, London
   Recorded: January 21, 1970

39 **HONKY CAT** *John/Taupin 5:12 (A)*
   SIXTY YEARS ON *John/Taupin 4:30 (B)*
   DJM DJS 10903 (UK). Released September 18, 1978
   Producer: Gus Dudgeon
   Studio: Strawberry Studios, Château D'Hierouville,
   France *(A)* Trident Studios, London *(B)*
   Recorded: January 1972 *(A)* January 1970 *(B)*

40 **COUNTRY COMFORT** *John/Taupin 5:00 (A)*
   CROCODILE ROCK *John/Taupin 3:34 (B)*
   DJM DJS 10904 (UK). Released September 18, 1978
   Producer: Gus Dudgeon
   Studio: Trident Studios, London *(A)* Strawberry
   Studios, Château D'Hierouville, France *(B)*
   Recorded: June 1970 *(A)* June 1972 *(B)*

41 **ROCKET MAN (I THINK IT'S GONNA BE A
   LONG LONG TIME)** *John/Taupin 4:35 (A)*
   DANIEL *John/Taupin 3:52 (B)*
   DJM DJS 10905 (UK). Released September 18, 1978
   Producer: Gus Dudgeon
   Studio: Strawberry Studios, Château

D'Hierouville, France
Recorded: January 1972 *(A)* June 1972 *(B)*

42 **SWEET PAINTED LADY** *John/Taupin 3:50 (A)*
   GOODBYE YELLOW BRICK ROAD *John/Taupin 3:13 (B)*
   DJM DJS 10906 (UK). Released September 18, 1978
   Producer: Gus Dudgeon
   Studio: Strawberry Studios, Château
   D'Hierouville, France
   Recorded: May 1973

43 **PHILADELPHIA FREEDOM** *John/Taupin 5:38 (A)*
   LUCY IN THE SKY WITH DIAMONDS
   Lennon/McCartney 5:58
   DJM DJS 10911 (UK). Released September 18, 1978
   Producer: Gus Dudgeon
   Studio: Caribou Ranch, Colorado, USA
   Recorded: June/July 1974 *(A)* Sept/October 1974 *(B)*

44 **CANDLE IN THE WIND** *John/Taupin 3:50 (A)*
   **I FEEL LIKE A BULLET (IN THE GUN OF
   ROBERT FORD)** *John/Taupin 5:30 (B)*
   DJM DJS 10908 (UK). Released September 18, 1978
   Producer: Gus Dudgeon
   Studio: Strawberry Studios, Château D'Hierouville,
   France *(A)* Caribou Ranch, Colorado, USA *(B)*
   Recorded: May 1973 *(A)* June/July 1975 *(B)*

45 **DON'T LET THE SUN GO DOWN ON ME**
   John/Taupin 5:33 (A)
   SOMEONE SAVED MY LIFE TONIGHT
   John/Taupin 3:09 (B)
   DJM DJS 10907 (UK). Released September 18, 1978
   Producer: Gus Dudgeon
   Studio: Caribou Ranch, Colorado, USA
   Recorded: January 1974 *(A)* June 1974 *(B)*

46 **THE BITCH IS BACK** *John/Taupin 3:40 (A)*
   GROW SOME FUNK OF YOUR OWN *John/Taupin/
   Johnstone 4:45 (B)*

DJM DJS 10909 (UK). Released September 18, 1978
Producer: Gus Dudgeon
Studio: Caribou Ranch, Colorado, USA
Recorded: January 1974 *(A)* June/July 1975 *(B)*

47 **ISLAND GIRL** *John/Taupin 3:46 (A)*
SATURDAY NIGHT'S ALRIGHT FOR FIGHTING
John/Taupin 4:55 (B)
DJM DJS 10910 (UK).
Released September 18, 1978
Producer: Gus Dudgeon
Studio: Caribou Ranch, Colorado, USA *(A)*
Strawberry Studios, Château D'Hierouville,
France *(B)*
Recorded: June/July 1975 *(A)* May 1973 *(B)*

48 **PINBALL WIZARD** *Townshend 5:14 (A)*
BENNY & THE JETS *John/Taupin 5:10 (B)*
DJM DJS 10912 (UK).
Released September 18, 1978
Producer: Gus Dudgeon
Studio: Ramport Studio, London *(A)* Strawberry
Studios, Château D'Hierouville, France *(B)*
Recorded: April 1974 *(A)* May 1973 *(B)*

49 **PART-TIME LOVE** *John/Osborne 3:12 (A)*
I CRY AT NIGHT *John/Taupin 3:10 (B)*
Rocket XPRESS I (UK). Released October 4, 1978
Producer: Elton John/Clive Franks
Studio: The Mill at Cookham, Berks.
Recorded: March 1978

50 **SONG FOR GUY** *John 5:01 (A)*
LOVESICK *John/Taupin 3:55 (B)*
Rocket XPRESS 5 (UK). Released November 28, 1978
Producer: Elton John/Clive Franks
Studio: The Mill at Cookham, Berks.
Recorded: 1978

51 **ARE YOU READY FOR LOVE** *T. Bell/L. Bell/*
James 5:05 Pt. I (A)

ARE YOU READY FOR LOVE *T. Bell/L. Bell
James 3:26 Pt. II (B)*
Rocket XPRESS 13 (UK) 7″ Version. Released
April 30, 1979
Producer: Thom Bell
Studio: Sigma & Sound Studios, Philadelphia *(A)*
Kay Smith Studio, Seattle *(B)*
Recorded: October 1977

52 **ARE YOU READY FOR LOVE** *C. Bell/T. Bell/
C. James 8:31 (A)*
THREE WAY LOVE AFFAIR *T. Bell/C. James 5:31 (B)*
MAMA CAN'T BUY YOU LOVE *T. Bell/
C. James 4:03 (C)*
Rocket XPRESS 13-12 (UK). 12″ Version.
Released April 30, 1979
Producer: Thom Bell
Studio: Sigma & Sound Studios, Philadelphia *(A)*
Kay Smith Studio, Seattle *(B,C)*
Recorded: October 1977

53 **MAMA CAN'T BUY YOU LOVE** *Bell/James 4:03 (A)*
STRANGERS *John/Osborne 4:40 (B)*
Rocket XPRESS 20 (UK). Released August 1979
Producer: Thom Bell *(A)* Elton John/Clive Franks *(B)*
Studio: Kay Smith Studio, Seattle *(A)* The Mill at
Cookham, Berks *(B)*
Recorded: October 1977 *(A)* March 1978 *(B)*
This 45 was pressed and ready for release in the UK
after the success of 'Mama Can't Buy You Love' in
the USA, but was withdrawn in favour of 'Victim of
Love' XPRESS 21.

54 **VICTIM OF LOVE** *P. Bellotte/Sylvester Le Vay/
J. Rix 3:18 (A)*
STRANGERS *John/Osborne 4:40 (B)*
Rocket XPRESS 21 (UK). Released September 14,
1979
Producer: Pete Bellotte *(A)* Elton John/
Clive Franks *(B)*

Studio: Musicland, Munich *(A)* The Mill at Cookham, Berks *(B)*
Recorded: August 1979 *(A)* March 1978 *(B)*

55 **JOHNNY B. GOODE** *C. Berry 8:06 (A)*
THUNDER IN THE NIGHT *Bellotte/Hoffmann 4:40 (B)*
Rocket XPRESS 24-12 12″ Version (UK).
Released December 1979
Producer: Pete Bellotte
Studio: Musicland, Munich
Recorded:August 1979

56 **JOHNNY B. GOODE** *C. Berry 3:22 (A)*
THUNDER IN THE NIGHT *Bellotte/Hoffmann 4:40 (B)*
Rocket XPRESS 24 (UK). 7″ Version.
Released December 1979
Producer: Pete Bellotte
Studio: Musicland, Munich
Recorded: August 1979

57 **LITTLE JEANNIE** *John/Osborne 5:18 (A)*
CONQUER THE SUN *John/Osborne 4:16 (B)*
Rocket XPRESS 32 (UK). Released May 1, 1980
Producer: Elton John/Clive Franks
Studio: Superbear Studios, Nice
Recorded: August 1979

58 **SARTORIAL ELOQUENCE** *John/T. Robinson 4:44 (A)*
WHITE MAN DANGER *John/Taupin 6:21 (B)*
CARTIER *Dinah Card/Carte Blanche 0:47 (C)*
Rocket XPRESS 41 (UK). Released August 5, 1980
Producer: Elton John/Clive Franks
Studio: Superbear Studios, Nice *(A)*
Recorded: August 1979 *(A,B)*

59 **HARMONY** *John/Taupin 2:50 (A)*
MONA LISAS AND MAD HATTERS
John/Taupin 5:00 (B)
DJM DJS 10961 (UK). Released November 1, 1980
Producer: Gus Dudgeon
Studio: Strawberry Studios, Château
D'Hierouville, France
Recorded: May 1973 *(A)* January 1972 *(B)*

60 **DEAR GOD** *John/Osborne 3:45 (A)*
TACTICS *John 2:45 (B)*
Rocket XPRESS 45 (UK). Released November
14, 1980
Producer: Elton John/Clive Franks
Studio: Superbear Studios, Nice
Recorded: August 1979

61 **DEAR GOD** *John/Osborne 3:45 (A)*
TACTICS *John 2:42 (B)*
STEAL AWAY CHILD *John/Osborne 3:00 (C)*

LOVE SO COLD *John/Taupin 3:53 (D)*
Rocket ELTON 1 (UK). 2 x 7".
Released November 14, 1980
Producer: Elton John/Clive Franks
Studio: Superbear Studios, Nice
Recorded: August 1979 *(A)*

62 **I SAW HER STANDING THERE**
Lennon/McCartney 3:05 (A)
**WHATEVER GETS YOU THROUGH THE
NIGHT** *Lennon 3:05 (B)*
LUCY IN THE SKY WITH DIAMONDS
Lennon/McCartney 5:40 (C)
DJM DJS 10965 (UK). Released March 13, 1981
Producer: Gus Dudgeon
Studio: Live from Madison Square Garden
Recorded: November 28, 1974

63 **NOBODY WINS** *John/Osborne 3:46 (B)*
FOOLS IN FASHIONS *John/Taupin 4:12*
Rocket XPRESS 54 (UK). Released May 8, 1981
Producer: Chris Thomas *(A)* Elton John/Clive Franks
Studio: Sunset Sound, Los Angeles
Recorded: August 1979-March 1980

64 **JUST LIKE BELGIUM** *John/Taupin 4:00*
**CAN'T GET OVER GETTING OVER LOSING
YOU** *John/Osborne 4:05*
Released July 3, 1981
Producer: Chris Thomas **(A)**
Elton John/Clive Franks *(B)*
Studio: Sunset Sound, Los Angeles *(A)*
Superbear Studios, Nice
Recorded: August 1979-March 1980

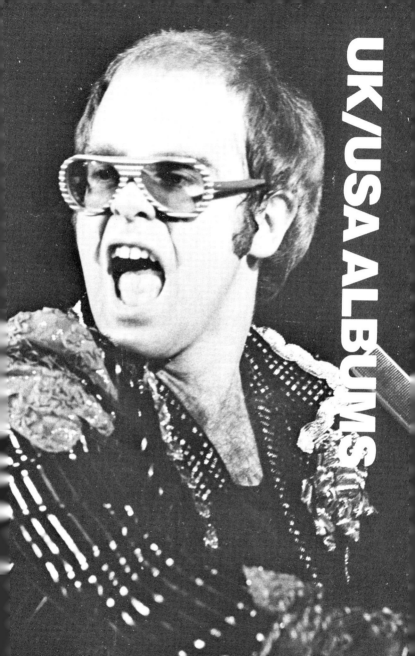

UK/USA ALBUMS

In terms of record sales in America throughout the seventies, it is doubtful whether there has been as successful an artist as Elton John.

By 1978 he had notched up twelve platinum albums and ten gold singles. The first of these gold singles, also his first American No. 1, was 'Crocodile Rock'.

In 1971 the album "Elton John" went gold in the States. Two singles were released from this album. 'Border Song' was one and the other, according to the record company, Uni, should have been 'Take Me To The Pilot'. However, American DJ's flipped for 'Your Song' which became the 'A' side by popular acclaim. (The Matrix number on the Uni pressing 45 shows 'Your Song' as the 'B' side). Both these records were released in 1970 although 'Border Song' had been released earlier on the "CONGRESS" label.

1971 heralded the release of four Elton John albums, and over-exposure threatened. This could have meant the destruction of his career in America, but he side-stepped disaster and overcame his problems in true superstar style.

"Honky Chateau" was Elton's first chart topping album and stayed at the number one spot for five weeks during 1972. Later that same year, saw, as mentioned above, his first US number one single from the shortly to be released LP "Don't Shoot Me I'm Only The Piano Player". Both album and single were the first issues on the new label in America for Elton, MCA. Original pressings were on black labels but later came the more familiar rainbow label.

'Don't Shoot Me' was actually released at the beginning of 1973, and a second single – 'Daniel' fell just short of being Elton's second number one. It reached number two in the US charts in April.

Elton released three more singles during 1973. Two were taken from his current album – a double LP entitled "Goodbye Yellow Brick Road" – and were the title track and 'Saturday Night's Alright For Fighting'. The third was a festive offering for the season called 'Step Into Christmas', which reached number one in a special Christmas chart.

Round about this time a Detroit based radio station called WJLB was getting a great response to the air-play it was giving to another track from the "Goodbye Yellow Brick Road" album, and was in fact creating a demand for the release of this number – 'Bennie & The Jets' – as a single. Elton never could see its potential as a single, but eventually agreed to its release, saying it was on the heads of those at MCA if it failed. In fact it turned out to be one of his biggest American sellers, gaining him his second number one single with sales of over two million copies. 'Bennie & The Jets' even reached number seventeen in the R&B charts, a very difficult area for a white pop singer to break into, and Elton appeared on the "Soul Train" television show with his hit song.

1974 seemed set in the same successful style. "Caribou" (named after the ranch in Colorado where it was recorded), hit number one and stayed there for four weeks. At this point along came the inevitable "Greatest Hits" compilation and highly successful it was too. It remained in the number one position for ten weeks.

This year also saw a slight change of direction for Elton. Up until now he had not released a single written by anyone but himself and Bernie Taupin – with the exception of 'Bluesology', foreign releases of 'Love Song' and 'Honky Tonk Woman' from earlier albums. This was changed when he released the Lennon/McCartney classic 'Lucy In The Sky With Diamonds' coupled with 'One Day At A Time', John Lennon's song from his LP "Mind Games". This single was Elton's third US number one, helped possibly by the fact that Dr Winston Boogie who plays along on the record is John Lennon.

28th November 1974. Madison Square Garden – New York. This date was to become one of the most memorable evenings in this venue's history, when John Lennon joined Elton on stage to sing three songs, 'Whatever Gets You Through The Night', 'Lucy In The Sky With Diamonds' and 'I Saw Her Standing There'. A never-to-be-forgotten experience for a thrilled audience.

1974 closed in grand style with Elton discovering that "Goodbye Yellow Brick Road" was the number one album of the year in America.

In 1975, in terms of albums, things got even bigger. "Greatest Hits" was the number one album of the year. Then came "Captain Fantastic and the Brown Dirt Cowboy", an autobiographical album, followed by "Rock of the Westies". These last two made their début at Number One in all three chart weeklies, *Cashbox, Billboard* and *Record World*. A 'first' since the 1940's. With the exception of "Empty Sky" which had just been issued for the first time in America, "Rock of the Westies" was Elton's seventh straight number one album success there. Quite an achievement by any standards.

Albums however, were not his only area of distinction. 1975 saw the climax of Elton's success in America which came to a head when an estimated 100,000 people saw him at the famous Dodger's Stadium in Los Angeles over two days in October to finish his West of the Rockies tour.

Elton's fifth number one American single came between the two last mentioned albums. It was taken from the "Rock of the Westies" LP and called 'Island Girl'. The fourth number one, which came out in February 1975, did not come from an album and was a single dedicated to tennis champion Billie-Jean King called 'Philadelphia Freedom' – it was coupled with live recording from the Madison Square Garden concert of 'I Saw Her Standing There', with John Lennon.

The first single release of 1976 was another track from "Rock of the Westies". Entitled 'I Feel Like a Bullet (In the Gun of Robert Ford)' and coupled with 'Grow Some Funk of Your Own', it was Elton's first single since 'Saturday Night's Alright For Fighting' in 1973 which did not immediately break into the US top ten. Was this a sign that perhaps the Americans had had just too much of Elton John? Well not exactly.

Early in 1976 he got together with Rocket Records artiste Kiki Dee on a duet. The result entitled 'Don't Go Breaking My Heart', released in June 1976 became his most successful single release, staying at number one for four weeks (longer than any of his previous records) and being named as the number two single of 1976.

Also in 1976 MCA released a second live album. Aptly titled "Here and There" it featured two concerts, one British and one American. Side one came from the Royal Festival Hall in London and side two was part of the now famous Madison Square Garden concert of 1974. This was the concert where John Lennon joined Elton on stage, but unfortunately the segment of the two of them singing three songs is missing from this LP, most likely due to contractual problems. However, even with this omission the album reached the number six position.

"Blue Moves", a double LP and Elton's first studio album for a year came next. Recorded in Canada it reached number three, and featured his last single of 1976 – 'Sorry Seems to be the Hardest Word'.

Elton's popularity began to fade in 1977. Here was an artist who had, at one point, been responsible for 2% of the entire world record sales. He wanted to take a new direction but his fans were not prepared to go with him. That year he did recording sessions with 'Spinners' producer, Thom Bell. These songs however, did not see the light of day until 1979, when three of them were released on a 12" single which had been remixed by Elton.

A fourth track from these sessions appeared on Elton's next album "A Single Man". This was 'Shine On Through'.* The album's title could have had double meaning in that it was also distinguished by being the first LP to be released without a single Bernie Taupin lyric.

In 1979 came the "Victim of Love" LP, which Elton

defends as being something he wanted to do and enjoyed recording. Disco however, did not appeal to his record buying public and the album was not a success.

At age 33 Elton's 21st LP excluding re-issues was released in 1980. The title was simple and straight to the point "21 at 33". 'Little Jeannie' was the single which became a hit.

There were varied writing partnerships on the record, including those of Elton and Judie Tzuke, Gary Osborne and the return of Bernie Taupin, whose absence was explained in the song 'Two Rooms at the End of the World.' Also featured were two songs written with Tom Robinson, 'Never Gonna Fall In Love Again' and 'Sartorial Eloquence'. (Titled 'Don't Ya Wanna Play This Game No More?' in the US.)

"21 at 33" and in particular the single release 'Sartorial Eloquence' became punctuation marks in Elton's career. 'Sartorial Eloquence' was the last single of 1980, taken from the last album of 1980, rounding off the year and the decade which had been so awesome in terms of success for Elton as a recording artist and performer. It was also the last release whilst with MCA in America.

His new USA label sees the release of his next album in 1981 called "The Fox" on Geffen Records.

*This version is not the Thom Bell mix but a new recording of the same song.

1 EMPTY SKY

DJM DJLPS 403 (UK). MCA 2130 (USA).
Released June 3, 1969 (UK). January 13, 1975 (USA).
Producer: Steve Brown
Studio: Dick James Studios, London
Recorded: December 1968 to April 1969
All compositions by Elton John/Bernie Taupin except *

(U.S.)

(U.K.)

Side One:
1. Empty Sky *8:29*
2. Val-Hala *4:09*
3. Western Ford Gateway *3:12*
4. Hymn 2000 *4:30*
Side Two:
5. Lady What's Tomorrow *3:06*
6. Sails *3:39*
7. The Scaffold *3:13*
8. Skyline Pigeon *3:31*
9. Gulliver-Hay Chewed * *John*
Reprise *John/Taupin 6:58*
Musicians: Elton, Caleb Quaye, Tony Murray, Roger
Pope, Don Fay, Graham Vickery, Nigel Ollson,
Clive Franks
Engineer: Frank Owen

2 ELTON JOHN

DJM DJLPS 406 (UK). UNI 73090 (USA).
Released April 10, 1970 (UK). July 22, 1970 (USA).
Producer: Gus Dudgeon

Studio: Trident Studios, London
Recorded: January 1970
All compositions by Elton John/Bernie Taupin
Side One:
1. Your Song *4:00*
2. I Need You To Turn To *2:30*
3. Take Me To The Pilot *3:48*
4. No Shoe Strings on Louise *3:30*
5. First Episode at Hienton *4:52*
Side Two:
6. Sixty Years On *4:33*
7. Border Song *3:19*
8. The Greatest Discovery *4:11*
9. The Cage *3:28*
10. The King Must Die *5:09*
Musicians: Elton, Barry Morgan, Dave Richmond, Frank
Clark, Colin Green, Clive Hicks, Roland Harker, Skaila
Kanga, Alan Weighll, Caleb Quaye, Alan Parker, D.
Lopez, Diana Lewis, Brian Dee, Terry Cox, Tex Navarra,
Les Hurdie, Paul Buckmaster, Barbara Moore*,
Madelaine Bell*, Leslie Duncan*, Kay Garner*, Tony
Burrows*, Tony Hazzard*, Roger Cook*.
* Backing Vocals
Engineer: Robin Geoffrey Cable
Arranged & Conducted: Paul Buckmaster

3. **TUMBLEWEED CONNECTION**
DJM DJLPS 410 (UK). UNI 73096 (USA).
Released October 30, 1970 (UK). January 4, 1971
(USA).
Producer: Gus Dudgeon
Studio: Trident Studios, London
Recorded: March 1970
All compositions by Elton John/Bernie Taupin except *
Leslie Duncan.
Side One:
1. Ballad of a Well Known Gun *4:59*
2. Come Down in Time *3:24*
3. Country Comfort *5:07*
4. Son of Your Father *3:46*
5. My Father's Gun *6:19*

Side Two
6. Where to Now St Peter *4:12*
7. Love Song* *3:39*
8. Amoreena *5:02*
9. Talking Old Soldiers *4:02*
10. Burn Down the Mission *6:20*
Musicians: Elton, Caleb Quaye, Roger Pope, Dave Glover, Barry Morgan, Herbie Flowers, Chris Laurence, Robin Jones, Mike Egan, Les Thatcher, Brian Dee, Gordon Huntley, J. Van Derek, Ian Duck, Dee Murray, Nigel Ollson, Skaila Kanga, Karl Jenkins.
Backing Vocals: Dusty Springfield, Madelaine Bell, Kay Garner, Lesley Duncan, Tony Hazzard, Tony Burrows, Sue & Sunny, Tammi Hunt, Dee, Nigel.
Arranged: Paul Buckmaster
Engineer: Robin G Cable

4 17.11.70 (UK). 11.17.70 (USA).
DJM DJLPS 414 (UK). UNI 98105 (USA).
Released April 1971 (UK). May 10, 1971 (USA).
Producer: Gus Dudgeon
Studio: A & R Studios, New York
Remixed (US version) Trident Studios, London (UK version) Dick James Studios, London
Recorded: November 17, 1970
All compositions by Elton John/Bernie Taupin unless stated
Side One
1. Take Me To The Pilot *6:43*
2. Honky Tonk Woman *(Jagger/Richard)* *4:09*
3. Sixty Years On *8:05*
4. Can I Put You On *6:38*
Side Two:
5. Bad Side Of The Moon *4:30*
6. Burn Down The Mission *18:20*
Including Medley
My Baby Left Me *A. Crudup*
Get Back *Lennon/McCartney*
Musicians: Elton, Nigel Ollson, Dee Murray
Engineer: Phil Ramones

5 **FRIENDS** (Soundtrack LP)
Paramount SPFL269 (UK). Paramount PAS6004
(USA). Released April 1971 (UK). March 5,
1971 (USA).
Producer: Gus Dudgeon. Executive Producer: John
Gilbert
Studio: Trident Studios, London
Recorded: October 1970
All compositions by Elton John/Bernie Taupin except (*)
A Poem by Richard Le Gallienne
* Introductions composed by Paul Buckmaster
XX Composed by Paul Buckmaster

Side One:
1. Friends *2:20*
2. Honey Roll *3:00*
3. *Variations on Friends *1:45*
4. Theme (The First Kiss) Seasons *3:52*
5. *Variations On Michelles Song *2:44*
6. Can I Put You On *5:52*
Side Two:
7. Michelles Song *4:16*
8. * (*) I Meant To Do My Work Today *1:33*
(A Day In The Country)
9. XX Four Moods *10:56*
10. Seasons Reprise *1:33*
Musicians: Elton, Nigel Ollson; Dee Murray; Caleb
Quaye; Rex Morris; Paul Buckmaster.
Backing Vocals: Liza Strike, Leslie Duncan,
Madelaine Bell
Arranged & Conducted: Paul Buckmaster
Engineer: Robin Geoffrey Cable
Notes: This LP was reissued in the UK on Anchor
Records ABCL 5082 and in the US on Pickwick Records
Notes: Original title for this film was to be "Intimate
Games"

6 **MADMAN ACROSS THE WATER**
DJM DJLPH 420 (UK). UNI 93120 (USA).
Released November 5, 1971 (UK). November 15,

1971 (USA)
Producer: Gus Dudgeon
Studio: Trident Studios, London
Recorded: August 9-14, 1971 except 2 & 9,
February 27, 1971
All compositions by Elton John/Bernie Taupin

Side One:
1. Tiny Dancer *6:12*
2. Levon *5:37*
3. Razor Face *4:46*
4. Madman Across the Water *5:22*
Side Two:
5. Indian Sunset *6:45*
6. Holiday Inn *4:22*
7. Rotten Peaches *5:14*
8. All the Nasties *5:08*
9. Goodbye *1:48*
Musicians: Elton, Roger Pope, David Glover, Caleb
Quaye, BJ Cole, D. Johnstone, Barry Morgan, Brian
Odgers, Brian Dee, Les Thatcher, Rick Wakeman, Jack
Ems, Terry Cox, Herbie Flowers, Ray Cooper, Chris
Spedding, Diana Lewis, Chris Lauren.
Backing Vocals: Leslie Duncan, Sue & Sunny, Barry
St John, Liza Strike, Roger Cook, Tony Burrows, Terry
Steele, Dee Murray, Nigel Ollson.
Arranged and Conducted: Paul Buckmaster
Backing Vocals: Liza Strike, Lesley Duncan/Madelaine
Bell.
Engineer: Robin Geoffrey Cable

7 **HONKY CHATEAU**
DJM DJLPH 423 (UK). UNI 93135 (USA).
Released May 19, 1972 (UK). May 26, 1972 (USA).
Producer: Gus Dudgeon
Studio: Strawberry Studios, Château D'Hierouville,
France. Remixed at Trident Studios, London
Recorded: January 1972
All compositions by Elton John/Bernie Taupin
Side One:
1. Honky Cat *5:12*

2. Mellow *5:30*
3. I Think I'm Gonna Kill Myself *3:32*
4. Suzie (Dramas) *3:24*
5. Rocket Man (I Think It's Going To Be A Long Long Time) *4:40*
Side Two
6. Salvation *3:26*
7. Slave *4:20*
8. Amy *4:02*
9. Mona Lisas & Mad Hatters *5:00*
10. Hercules *5:20*

Musicians: Elton, Dee Murray, Davey Johnstone, Nigel Ollson, Jacques Bolognesi, Ivan Jullien, J L Cautemps, Alain Hatot, Jean-Luc Ponty, David Henschel, Ray Cooper, Legs Larry Smith.
Backing Vocals: Madelaine Bell, Liza Strike, Larry Steel, Tony Hazzard
Engineer: Ken Scott

8 **DON'T SHOOT ME I'M ONLY THE PIANO PLAYER**
DJM DJLPH 427 (UK). MCA 2100 (USA).
Released January 26 1973 (UK). January 22, 1973 (USA).
Producer: Gus Dudgeon
Studio: Strawberry Studios, Château D'Hierouville,France.
Remixed at Trident Studios, London
Recorded: June/July 1972

All compositions by Elton John/Bernie Taupin
Side One
1. Daniel *3:52*
2. Teacher I Need You *4:08*
3. Elderberry Wine *3:34*
4. Blues For My Baby And Me *5:38*
5. Midnight Creeper *3:53*
Side Two:
6. Have Mercy On The Criminal *5:55*
7. I'm Gonna Be A Teenage Idol *3:55*
8. Texan Love Song *3:33*
9. Crocodile Rock *3:56*
10. High Flying Bird *4:10*
Musicians: Elton, Dee Murray,
Nigel Ollson, Davey Johnstone, Ken Scott,
J. Bolognesi, I. Jullien,
J L Chautemps, Alain Hutot.
Engineer: Ken Scott

9 **GOODBYE YELLOW BRICK ROAD**
DJM DJLPD 1001/2 (UK). MCA 210003 (USA)
Released October 5, 1973 (UK). October 5,
1973 (USA).
Producer: Gus Dudgeon
Studio: Strawberry Studios, Château D'Hierouville,
France. Remixed at Trident Studios, London
Recorded: May 1973
All compositions by Elton John/Bernie Taupin
Side One:
1. Funeral For A Friend *11.05*
2. Love Lies Bleeding
3. Candle in the Wind *3:41*
4. Bennie & The Jets *5:10*
Side Two:
5. Goodbye Yellow Brick Road *3:13*
6. This Song Has No Title *2:18*
7. Grey Seal *4:03*
8. Jamaica Jerk Off *3:36*
9. I've Seen That Movie Too *5:59*
Side Three:
10. Sweet Painted Lady *3:52*

11. The Ballad of Danny Bailey 1909-34 *4:24*
12. Dirty Little Girl *5:03*
13. All the Young Girls Love Alice *5:13*
Side Four:
14. Your Sister Can't Twist (But She Can Rock & Roll) *2:41*
15. Saturday Night's Alright For Fighting *4:50*
16. Roy Rogers *4:10*
17. Social Disease *3:45*
18. Harmony *2:49*
Musicians: Elton, Dee Murray, Nigel Ollson, Davey Johnstone, David Henschel, Leroy Gomez, Del Newman
Engineer: David Henschel

10 **CARIBOU**
DJM DJLPS 439 (UK). MCA 2116 (USA).
Released June 28, 1974 (UK). June 24, 1974 (USA).
Producer: Gus Dudgeon
Studio: Caribou Ranch, Colorado, USA. Remixed Trident Studios, London. Recorded: January 1974
All compositions by Elton John/Bernie Taupin
Side One:
1. The Bitch is Back *3:42*
2. Pinky *3:53*
3. Grimsby *3:47*
4. Dixie Lily *2:48*
5. Solar Prestige A Gammon *2:50*
6. You're So Static *4:49*
Side Two:
7. I've Seen the Saucers *4:45*
8. Stinker *5:16*
9. Don't Let the Sun Go Down on Me *5:33*
10. Ticking *7:34*
Musicians: Elton John, Dee Murray, Nigel Ollson, Davey Johnstone, Ray Cooper, Dave Henschel, Lenny Pickett, Stephen Kupka, Emilio Castillo, Mic Gillette, Greg Adams, Chester Thompson, Del Newman.
Backing Vocals: Clydie King, Sherlie Mathews, Jessie Mae Smith, Dusty Springfield, Carl Wilson, Bruce Johnston, Toni Tennille, Billy Hinsche.
Engineer: Clive Franks

11 GREATEST HITS

DJM DJLPH 422 (UK). MCA 2128 (USA).
Released November 8, 1974 (UK). November 4,
1974 (USA).
Producer: Gus Dudgeon
Studio: Various
Recorded:
All compositions by Elton John/Bernie Taupin

Side One:
1. Your Song *4:00*
2. Daniel *3:52*
3. Honky Cat *5:12*
4. Goodbye Yellow Brick Road *3:13*
5. Saturday Night's Alright for Fighting *4:55*
Side Two:
6. Rocket Man *4:40*
7. Candle in the Wind *3:41*
8. Don't Let the Sun Go Down On Me *5:33*
9. Border Song *3:19*
10. Crocodile Rock *3:56*
Note: USA Pressing Features "Benny and The Jets"
instead of "Candle in the Wind."

12 CAPTAIN FANTASTIC AND THE BROWN DIRT COWBOY

DJM DJLPX 1 (UK). MCA 2142 (USA).
Released May 23, 1975 (UK) May 19, 1975 (USA)
Producer: Gus Dudgeon

Studio: Caribou Ranch, Colorado, USA
Remixed Marquee Studios, London
Recorded: June/July 1974
All compositions by Elton John/Bernie Taupin
Side One:
1. Captain Fantastic & The Brown Dirt Cowboy *5:45*
2. Tower of Babel *4:28*
3. Bitter Fingers *4:32*
4. Tell Me When the Whistle Blows *4:20*
5. Someone Saved My Life Tonight *6:45*
Side Two:
6. (Gotta Get A) Meal Ticket *4:00*
7. Better Off Dead *2:35*
8. Writing *3:38*
9. We All Fall In Love Sometimes *4:15*
10. Curtains *6:12*
*First 2,000 copies specially pressed on brown vinyl
Musicians: Elton, Dee Murray, Nigel Ollson,
Davey Johnstone, Ray Cooper, Dave Henschel
Engineer: Jeff Guercio
Also issued in 1978 as a Picture Disc DJM (UK)
DJV 23000

13 **ROCK OF THE WESTIES**
DJM DJLPH 464 (UK). MCA 2163 (USA)
Released October 4, 1975 (UK). October 20,
1975 (USA)
Producer: Gus Dudgeon
Studio: Caribou Ranch, Colorado, USA
Remixed at Trident Studios, London
Recorded: June/July 1975
All compositions by Elton John/Bernie Taupin
unless stated
Side One:
1. Medley (Yell Help, Wednesday Night, Ugly)
(John/Taupin/Johnstone) 6:30
2. Dan Dare (Pilot of the Future) *3:25*
3. Island Girl *2:45*
4. Grow Some Funk of Your Own *4:45*
5. I Feel Like a Bullet (In the Gun of
Robert Ford) *5:30*

Side Two:
6. Street Kids *6:30*
7. Hard Luck Story *(Orson/Blanche) 5:05*
8. Feed Me *4:00*
9. Billy Bones and the White Bird *4:25*
Musicians: Elton, Kenny Passerelli, Roger Pope,
Davey Johnstone, Caleb Quaye, Ray Cooper,
James Newton-Howard
Backing Vocals: Labelle, Kiki Dee, Kenny, Davey,
Ann Orson, Caleb
Engineer: Jeff Guercio

14 **HERE AND THERE**
DJM DJLPH 473 (UK), MCA 2197 (USA)
Released April 30, 1976 (UK). May 3, 1976 (USA)
Producer: Gus Dudgeon
Studio: Side 1 – recorded live at
The Royal Festival Hall, London
Side 2 – recorded live at
Madison Square Garden, New York
Remixed at Marquee Studios, London
Recorded: Side 1 – May 18, 1974
Side 2 – November 28, 1974
All compositions by Elton John/Bernie Taupin except
*Leslie Duncan
Side One:
1. Skyline Pigeon *4:44*
2. Border Song *3:23*
3. Honky Cat *7:32*
4. Love Song* *5:41*
5. Crocodile Rock *4:04*
Side Two:
6. Funeral For A Friend *11:47*
7. Love Lies Bleeding
8. Rocket Man *4:48*
9. Benny & the Jets *6:17*
10. Take Me to the Pilot *5:55*
Musicians: Side 1 – Elton, Dee Murray,
Nigel Ollson, Davey Johnstone, Ray Cooper,
The Muscle Shoals Horns

Side 2 – Elton, Dee, Nigel, Davey
Backing Vocals: Leslie Duncan, on Love Song.
Engineers: Phil Dunne, Gus Dudgeon

15 **BLUE MOVES**
Rocket/EMI ROSP1 (UK). Rocket/MCA 211004 (USA)
Released October 22, 1976 (UK).
October 28, 1976 (USA)
Producer: Gus Dudgeon
Studio: Eastern Sound, Toronto
Remixed at Marquee Studios, London
Recorded: March 1976
All compositions by Elton John/
Bernie Taupin except
*Caleb Quaye
Side One:
1. Your Starter for . . .* *1:25*
2. Tonight *8:02*
3. One Horse Town *John/Taupin Howard 5:47*
4. Chameleon *5:27*
Side Two:
5. Boogie Pilgrim *John/Taupin*
Johnstone/Quaye 6:03
6. Cage the Songbird *John/Taupin/Johnstone 3:28*
7. Crazy Water *5:42*
8. Shoulder Holster *4:20*
Side Three:
9. Sorry Seems to be the Hardest Word *3:43*
10. Out of the Blue *6:10*
11. Between Seventeen & Twenty *John/Taupin/Johnstone/*
Quaye 5:10
12. The Wide Eyed & Laughing *John/Taupin/Johnstone/*
Quaye 3:20
13. Someone's Final Song *4:00*
Side Four:
14. Where's the Shoorah *4:10*
15. If There's a God in Heaven (What's He
Waiting For?) *John/Taupin/Johnstone 4:20*
16. Idol *4:10*
17. Theme From a non-existent TV Series *1:20*
18. Bite Your Lip (Get Up & Dance) *6:37*

Musicians: Elton, Kenny Passerelli, Roger Pope,
Caleb Quaye, Davey Johnstone, Ray Cooper,
James Newton Howard, Michael & Randy Brecher,
B. Rogers, D. Sanborn.
Martin Ford Orchestra, LSO, Carl Fortina,
Paul Buckmaster
Backing Vocals: Bruce Johnson, Toni Tennille,
Curt Becher, John Yoyce, Cindy Bullens,
Ron Hickun, Gene Morford, David Crosby,
Graham Nash, Joe Chemay, Cornerstone Baptist Choir,
Southern California Choir.
Engineer: Gus Dudgeon/John Stewart

16. GREATEST HITS VOLUME II
DJM DJLPH 20520 (UK) MCA 3027 (USA)
Released September 13, 1977 (UK).
October 1, 1977 (USA)
Producer: Gus Dudgeon
Studio: Various
Recorded:
All compositions by Elton John/Bernie Taupin except
*Orson/Blanche **Pete Townshend
***Lennon/McCartney
Side One:
1. The Bitch Is Back *3:42*
2. Lucy In the Sky With Diamonds*** *5:58*
3. Sorry Seems to be the Hardest Word *3:43*
4. Don't Go Breaking My Heart* *4:23*
5. Someone Saved My Life Tonight *6:45*
Side Two:
6. Philadelphia Freedom *5:38*
7. Island Girl *3:45*
8. Grow Some Funk of Your Own *John/Taupin/*
Johnstone 4:45
9. Benny & The Jets *5:10*
10. Pinball Wizard** *5:08*
Note: USA pressing features "Levon" *4:59* instead of
"Benny & The Jets" as Benny was included on Vol 1.

17 CANDLE IN THE WIND
St Michael 2094/0102 (UK).

Released January 1978 (UK).
Producer: Gus Dudgeon, *Stephen Brown
Studio: Various
Recorded:
All compositions by Elton John/Bernie Taupin
Side One:
1. Skyline Pigeon* (1969 Version)
2. Take Me To The Pilot
3. Burn Down the Mission
4. Teacher I Need You
5. Rocket Man
6. Don't Let The Sun Go Down On Me
7. Elderberry Wine
Side Two:
8. Bennie & The Jets
9. Midnight Creeper
10. Dan Dare (Pilot of the Future)
11. Someone Saved My Life Tonight
12. Better Off Dead
13. Grey Seal (original 1970 Version)
14. Candle In The Wind

Note: This album was released by CBS
Special Products for the Marks and Spencer
chain stores.

18 **ELTON JOHN LIVE**
Pickwick SHM 942 (UK). Released March 1, 1978
Producer: Gus Dudgeon

Studio: Same as "17.11.70" DJM DJLPS 414 (UK)
Recorded: See '17.11.70'

19 **LONDON AND NEW YORK (LIVE)**
Pickwick SHM 966 (UK). Released September 1,
1978 (UK)
Producer: Gus Dudgeon
Studio: Same as "Here And There"
DJM DJLPH 473 (UK)
Recorded: See "Here And There".

20 **A SINGLE MAN**
Rocket Train 1 (UK). MCA 3065 (USA).
Released October 16, 1978 (UK). October 1978 (USA).
Producer: Elton John/Clive Franks
Studio: The Mill at Cookham, Berks.
Recorded: January-September 1978
All compositions by Elton John/Gary Osborne except
*Elton John

Side One:
1. Shine On Through *3:40*
2. Return to Paradise *4:12*
3. I Don't Care *4:20*
4. Big Dipper *4:00*
5. It Ain't Gonna Be Easy *8:23*
Side Two:
6. Part-Time Love *3:12*

49

7. Georgia *4:47*
8. Shooting Star *2:43*
9. Madness *6:07*
10. Reverie* *0:52*
11. Song For Guy* *6:34*
Musicians: Elton, Steve Holly, Clive Franks, Ray Cooper,
Tim Renwick, Henry Lowther, Pat Halcox, John
Crocker, Jim Shepherd, Davey Johnstone, B.J. Cole,
Herbie Flowers, Paul Buckmaster.
Backing Vocals: Vicky Brown, Joanne Stone, Steve
Cange, Chris Thompson, Watford Football Club,
South Audley Street Girls Choir.
Engineer: Phil Dunne, Stuart Epps, Clive Franks
Also issued as a picture disc
MCAP 14951 (US)

21 **THE ELTON JOHN LIVE COLLECTION**
Pickwick PDA 047 (UK). Released February 5,
1979 (UK).
Producer: Gus Dudgeon
Studio: Record 1 is same as "17.11.70"
DJM DJLPS 414 (UK).
Record 2 is same as "Here And There"
DJM DJLPH 473 (UK).
Recorded:
1. See "17.11.70"
2. See "Here And There"

22 **EARLY YEARS**
DJM LSP 13833. Released August 1, 1979 (UK)
Producer: Gus Dudgeon except tracks 1, 2 & 3
Steve Brown
Studio: 1, 2 & 3 – Dick James Studios, London.
All other tracks Trident Studios, London
Recorded: 1968-1971
All compositions by Elton John/Bernie Taupin
Side One:
1. Lady Samantha
2. Skyline Pigeon
3. Empty Sky

4. Border Song
5. I Need You To Turn To
6. Sixty Years On

Side Two:
7. Country Comfort
8. Burn Down The Mission
9. Where To Now St Peter
10. Levon
11. Madman Across The Water
12. Friends
LP was available in Boxed Set LP 14512 DJM

23 **ELTON ROCKS**
DJM LSP 13834 (UK). Released August 1, 1979 (UK).
Producer: Gus Dudgeon
Studio: Various
Recorded:
All compositions Elton John/Bernie Taupin except
*Pete Townshend
Side One:
1. Saturday Night's Alright For Fighting
2. (Gotta Get A) Meal Ticket
3. Screw You
4. Teacher I Need You
5. Grow Some Funk Of Your Own
6. Grey Seal (1973 Version)
7. The Bitch Is Back
Side Two:
8. Crocodile Rock
9. The Cage
10. Elderberry Wine
11. Whenever You're Ready (We'll Go Steady Again)
12. Street Kids
13. Midnight Creeper
14. Pinball Wizard*
LP was available in Boxed Set LSP 14512 DJM

24 **MOODS**
DJM LSP 13835. Released August 1, 1979 (UK).
Producer: Gus Dudgeon

Studio: Various
Recorded:
All compositions by Elton John/Bernie Taupin except
*Lesley Duncan
Side One:
1. I Feel Like a Bullet (In The Gun of Robert Ford)
2. Mona Lisas & Mad Hatters
3. High Flying Bird
4. Tiny Dancer
5. The Greatest Discovery
6. Blues For My Baby & Me
Side Two:
7. Harmony
8. I've Seen That Movie Too
9. Pinky
10. It's Me That You Need
11. Indian Sunset
12. Sweet Painted Lady
13. Love Song*
LP was available in Boxed Set LSP 14512 DJM

25 **SINGLES**
DJM LSP 13836 (UK). Released August 1, 1979
Producer: Gus Dudgeon
Studio: Various
Recorded:
All compositions by Elton John/Bernie Taupin except
*Lennon/McCartney
Side One:
1. Your Song
2. Rocket Man
3. Honky Cat
4. Daniel
5. Goodbye Yellow Brick Road
6. Candle In The Wind
7. Don't Let The Sun Go Down On Me
Side Two:
8. Lucy In The Sky With Diamonds*
9. Philadelphia Freedom
10. Someone Saved My Life Tonight
11. Island Girl
12. Bennie & The Jets
LP was available in Boxed Set LSP 14512 DJM

26 **CLASSICS**
DJM LSP 13837. Released August 1, 1979
Producer: Gus Dudgeon
Studio: Various
Recorded:
All compositions by Elton John/Bernie Taupin
Side One:
1. Funeral For A Friend
2. Love Lies Bleeding

3. The Ballad of Danny Bailey 1909-34
4. Ticking
Side Two:
5. Texan Love Song
6. Captain Fantastic & The Brown Dirt Cowboy
7. We All Fall In Love Sometimes
8. Curtains
LP was available in Boxed Set LSP 14512 DJM

27 **VICTIM OF LOVE**
Rocket HSPD 125 (UK). MCA 5104 (USA).
Released October 13, 1979 (UK). October 1979 (USA)
Producer: Pete Bellotte
Studio: Musicland, Munich. Rusk Sound Studios,
Hollywood
Recorded: August 1979
1. Johnny B. Goode *Chuck Berry 8:06*
2. Warm Love In A Cold World *P. Bellotte/S. Wisnet/
G. Moll 3:22*
3. Born Bad *P. Bellotte/G. Bastow 6:20*
Side Two:
4. Thunder In The Night *P. Bellotte/M. Hoffmann 4:40*
5. Spotlight *Bellotte/Wisnet/G. Moll 4:22*
6. Street Boogie *Bellotte/Wisnet/G. Moll 3:53*
7. Victim Of Love *Bellotte/Le Vay/J. Rix 5:02*
Musicians: Keith Forsey, Marcus Miller, Craig Snyder,
Tim Cawsfield, Thor Baldursson, Roy Davies, Paulinno
Da Costa, Steve Lukather, Lenny Pickett.
Backing Vocals: Mike McDonald, Patrick Simmons,
Stephanie Spervill, Maxine Waters, Julia Waters.
Engineer: Peter Liedman
Notes: Album was originally to be titled "Thunder In
The Night"

28 **21 AT 33**
Rocket HSPD 126 (UK). MCA 5121 (USA).
Released May 13, 1980 (UK). May 1980 (USA).
Producer: Elton John/Clive Franks
Studio: Superbear Studios, Nice. Remixed at Sunset
Sound, Hollywood, USA

Recorded: August 1979
Side One:
1. Chasing The Crown *John/Taupin 5:36*
2. Little Jeannie *John/Osborne 5:18*
3. Sartorial Eloquence *John/Robinson 4:44*
4. Two Rooms At The End Of The World *John/Taupin 5:37*
Side Two:
5. White Lady White Powder *John/Taupin 4:35*
6. Dear God *John/Osborne 3:45*
7. Never Gonna Fall In Love Again *John/Robinson 4:07*
8. Take Me Back *John/Osborne 3:52*
9. Give Me The Love *John/Tzuke 5:19*

Musicians: Elton, Nigel Ollson, James Newton-Howard, Ritchie Zito, J. Horn, C. Findley, J. Hey, Dee Murray, Alvin Taylor, R. McBride, S. Lukather, V. Fieldman, Clive Franks, Lenny Castro, David Patch, Byron Berline, L. Hall, L. Williams, B. Reichenbach.
Backing Vocals: Bruce Johnson, Toni Tennille, Peter Noone, C. Becher, J. Joyce, J. Chemay, Glenn Frey, Tim Schmidt.
Engineers: Patrick Jaunead, Clive Franks

29 **LADY SAMANTHA**
DJM 22085 (UK). Released October 13, 1980 (UK)
Producer: Steve Brown tracks 6, 10, 13.
All other tracks Gus Dudgeon
Studio: Various

All compositions Elton John/Bernie Taupin
Side One:
1. Rock & Roll Madonna
2. Whenever You're Ready
(We'll Go Steady Again)
3. Bad Side Of The Moon
4. Jack Rabbit
5. Into The Old Man's Shoes
6. It's Me That You Need
7. Ho! Ho! Ho! Who'd Be A Turkey At Christmas
Side Two:
8. Skyline Pigeon
9. Screw You
10. Just Like Strange Rain
11. Grey Seal
12. The Honey Roll
13. Lady Samantha
14. Friends
Notes: This LP was originally available only as a tape.
Released on Precision Tapes/DJM issued in 1974
Cartridge: Y8DJL 301. Cassette: ZCDJL 301

30 **THE VERY BEST OF ELTON JOHN**
K.TEL NE1094 (UK). Released October 13, 1980 (UK)
Producer: Gus Dudgeon except Song For Guy,
Elton John/Clive Franks
Studio: Various
Recorded:
All compositions by Elton John/Bernie Taupin except
*Elton John **Ann Orson/Carte Blanche
Side One:
1. Your Song
2. Goodbye Yellow Brick Road
3. Daniel
4. Song For Guy*
5. Candle In The Wind
6. Friends
7. Tiny Dancer
8. Rocket Man (I Think It's Gonna Be
A Long Long Time)
Side Two:
9. Don't Go Breaking My Heart**
10. Sorry Seems To Be The Hardest Word
11. Border Song
12. Someone Saved My Life Tonight
13. Mona Lisas & Mad Hatters
14. Harmony
15. High Flying Bird
16. Don't Let The Sun Go Down On Me

31 **MILESTONES (1970-1980 A DECADE OF GOLD)**
K.TEL TU2640 (USA). Released November 1980 (USA)
Producer: Gus Dudgeon except *Thom Bell

Studio: Various
Recorded:
All compositions by Elton John/Bernie Taupin
unless stated

Side One:
1. Don't Go Breaking My Heart *Orson/Blanche*
2. Island Girl
3. The Bitch Is Back
4. Honky Cat
5. Bennie & The Jets
6. Someone Saved My Life Tonight
7. Don't Let The Sun Go Down On Me
8. Sorry Seems To Be The Hardest Word
Side Two:
9. Mama Can't Buy You Love **Bell/James*
10. Philadelphia Freedom
11. Crocodile Rock
12. Rocket Man
13. Daniel
14. Lucy In The Sky With Diamonds *Lennon/McCartney*
15. Your Song
16. Goodbye Yellow Brick Road

32 THE FOX
Rocket Train 16 (UK). Geffen GEF 49722 (US).
Released May 20, 1981. May 22, 1981 (US).
Producer: Chris Thomas. *By Elton John/Clive Franks

Studio: Sunset Sound, Davlen Studios, Village Recorders, Los Angeles, USA. Superbear, Nice, France. EMI, Abbey Road, London. Remixed – Wessex Studios London, Superbear, Los Angeles, USA.

Recorded: August 1979-March 1980

Side One:
1. Breaking Down The Barriers *John/Osborne 4.35*
2. Heart In The Right Place* *John/Osborne (5.15)*
3. Just Like Belgium *John/Taupin 4.05*
4. Nobody Wins *Jean Paul Dreau/Osborne 3.42*
5. Fascist Faces *John/Taupin 5.10*

Side Two:
6. a. Carla* *John 4.50* b. Etude *John* c. Fanfare *John/Newton Howard 1.30* d. Chloe *John/Osborne 4.35*
7. Heels Of The Wind *John/Taupin 3.34*
8. Elton's Song* *John/Tom Robinson 3.00*
9. The Fox *John/Taupin 5.12*

Musicians: Elton John; Nigel Olsson; Dee Murray; Ritchie Zito; Jim Horn; Stephanie Spruill; James Newton Howard; Alvin Taylor; Reggie McBride; Collette Bertrand; Mickey Raphael; London Symphony Orchestra; Cornerstone Baptist Church Choir.

Backing Vocals: Stephanie Spruill; Venette Gloud, Bill Bill Champlin; Tamara Matoesian; Gary Osborne; Max Gronthal; James Giltrap; John Lehman; Carl Carwell; Roy Galloway; Oren Waters; Ronald Baker; Chuck Cissel; Clarence Ford; Victor Feldman.

Engineers: Bill Price; Steve McManus; Peggy McCreary; Patrick Jaunead; Karen Siegel; John Kurlander; Jeremy Green.

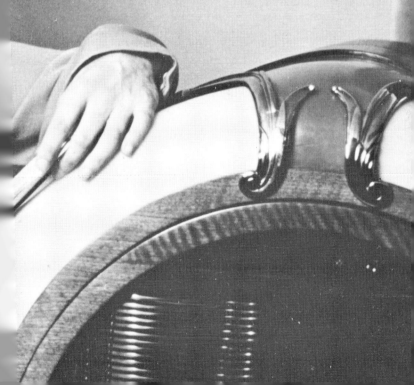

US SINGLES

1 **LADY SAMANTHA** *John/Taupin 3:03 (A)*
ALL ACROSS THE HAVENS *John/Taupin 3:50 (B)*
DJM 70008 (US). Released January 1969
Producer: Steve Brown
Studio: Dick James Studios, London
Recorded: December 1968
Note: This is the first known record to be released
by Elton in the USA.

2 **LADY SAMANTHA** *John/Taupin 3:03 (A)*
IT'S ME THAT YOU NEED *John/Taupin 4:04 (B)*
Congress C6017 (US). Released January 1970
Producer: Steve Brown
Studio: Dick James Studios, London *(A)* Olympic
Studio, London *(B)*
Recorded: December 1968 *(A)* April 10, 1969 *(B)*

3 **BORDER SONG** *John/Taupin 3:20 (A)*
BAD SIDE OF THE MOON *John/Taupin 3:12 (B)*
Congress C6022 (US). Released April 1970
Producer: Gus Dudgeon
Studio: Trident Studios, London
Recorded: January 1970

4 **FROM DENVER TO L.A.** *Lai/Shaper 2:01 (A)*
WARM SUMMER RAIN *Lai/Shaper 2:05 (B)*
Viking 1010 (US). Released 1970
Producer & Arranger: Christian Gaubert
Studio: Olympic Studios, London
Recorded: 1969
Notes: *(A)* Vocals credited to Elton Johns.
(B) Is by "The Barbara Moore Singers"
(Both sides taken from "The Games"
Soundtrack Album)

5 **BORDER SONG** *John/Taupin 3:20 (A)*
BAD SIDE OF THE MOON *John/Taupin 3:12 (B)*
UNI 55246 (US). Released September 1970
Producer: Gus Dudgeon
Studio: Trident Studios, London
Recorded: January 1970

6 **TAKE ME TO THE PILOT** *John/Taupin 3:43 (A)*
Matrix No. 534
YOUR SONG *John/Taupin 3:51 (B) Matrix No. 535*
UNI 55265 (US). Released October 26, 1970 (US)
Producer: Gus Dudgeon
Studio: Trident Studios, London
Recorded: January 1970
Note: Matrix Nos suggest that "Take Me To The
Pilot" was the intended 'A' Side. But US DJ's opted
for "Your Song".

7 **FRIENDS** *John/Taupin 2:29 (A)*
HONEY ROLL *John/Taupin 2:57 (B)*
UNI 55277 (US). Released March 5, 1971
Producer: Gus Dudgeon
Studio: Trident Studios, London
Recorded: October 1970

8 **LEVON** *John/Taupin 4:59 (A)*
GOODBYE *John/Taupin 1:45 (B)*
UNI 55314 (US). Mono. Released November 29, 1971
Producer: Gus Dudgeon
Studio: Trident Studios, London
Recorded: February 27, 1971

9 **TINY DANCER** *John/Taupin 6:12 (A)*
RAZOR FACE *John/Taupin 4:40 (B)*
UNI 55318 (US). Released February 7, 1972
Producer: Gus Dudgeon
Studio: Trident Studios, London
Recorded: August 9, 1971

10 **ROCKET MAN** *John/Taupin 4:35 (A)*
SUZIE (DRAMAS) *John/Taupin 3:25 (B)*
UNI 55328 (US). Released April 17, 1972
Producer: Gus Dudgeon
Studio: Strawberry Studios, Château
D'Hierouville, France
Recorded: January 1972

11 **HONKY CAT** *John/Taupin 5:12 (A)*
SLAVE *John/Taupin 4:20 (B)*
UNI 55343 (US). Released July 31, 1972
Producer: Gus Dudgeon
Studio: Strawberry Studios, Château
D'Hierouville, France
Recorded: January 1972

12 **CROCODILE ROCK** *John/Taupin 3:56 (A)*
ELDERBERRY WINE *John/Taupin 3:34 (B)*
MCA 40000 (US). Released November 20, 1972
Producer: Gus Dudgeon
Studio: Strawberry Studios, Château
D'Hierouville, France
Recorded: June 1972

13 **DANIEL** *John/Taupin 3:52 (A)*
SKYLINE PIGEON *John/Taupin 3:45 (B)*
MCA 40046 (US). Released March 26, 1973
Producer: Gus Dudgeon
Studio: Strawberry Studios, Château
D'Hierouville, France
Recorded: June 1972

14 SATURDAY NIGHT'S ALRIGHT FOR FIGHTING
John/Taupin 4:55 (A)
JACK RABBIT *John/Taupin 1:50 (B)*
WHENEVER YOU'RE READY (WE'LL GO
STEADY AGAIN) *John/Taupin 2:50 (C)*
MCA 40105 (US). Released July 16, 1973
Producer: Gus Dudgeon
Studio: Strawberry Studios, Château
D'Hierouville, France
Studio: May 1973

15 GOODBYE YELLOW BRICK ROAD
John/Taupin 3:13 (A)
YOUNG MAN'S BLUES *John/Taupin 4:41 (B)**
MCA 40148 (US). Released October 15, 1973
Producer: Gus Dudgeon
Studio: Strawberry Studios, Château
D'Hierouville, France
Recorded: May 1973
*Because of its strong connotation in American slang
"Screw You" was retitled in the USA.

16 STEP INTO XMAS *John/Taupin 4:30 (A)*
HO! HO! HO! WHO'D BE A TURKEY
AT CHRISTMAS *John/Taupin 4:04 (B)*
MCA 65018 (US). Released November 26, 1973
Producer: Gus Dudgeon
Studio: Trident Studios, London
Recorded: November 1973

17 BENNIE & THE JETS *John/Taupin 5:10 (A)*
HARMONY *John/Taupin 2:49 (B)*
MCA 40198 (US). Released February 4, 1974
Producer: Gus Dudgeon
Studio: Strawberry Studios, Château
D'Hierouville, France
Recorded: May 1973

18 DON'T LET THE SUN GO DOWN ON ME
John/Taupin 5:33 (A)
SICK CITY *John/Taupin 5:22 (B)*
MCA 40259 (US). Released May 1974
Producer: Gus Dudgeon
Studio: Caribou Ranch, Colorado, USA
Recorded: January 1974 *(A)* April 1974 *(B)*

19 THE BITCH IS BACK *John/Taupin 3:42 (A)*
COLD HIGHWAY *John/Taupin 3:25 (B)*
MCA 40297 (US). Released September 3, 1974
Producer: Gus Dudgeon
Studio: Caribou Ranch, Colorado, USA
Recorded: January 1974

20 **LUCY IN THE SKY WITH DIAMONDS**
Lennon/McCartney 5:58 (A)
ONE DAY AT A TIME *Lennon 3:17 (B)*

MCA 40344 (US). Released November 18, 1974
Producer: Gus Dudgeon
Studio: Caribou Ranch, Colorado, USA
Recorded: July 1974

21 **PHILADELPHIA FREEDOM** *John/Taupin 5:38 (A)*
I SAW HER STANDING THERE
Lennon/McCartney 3:53 (B)
MCA 40364 (US). Released February 24, 1975
Producer: Gus Dudgeon
Studio: Caribou Ranch, Colorado, USA *(A)*
Madison Square Garden, New York *(B)*
Recorded: June/July 1974 *(A)* November 28, 1974
Live Concert recording with John Lennon *(B)*

22 **SOMEONE SAVED MY LIFE TONIGHT**
John/Taupin 6:45 (A)
HOUSE OF CARDS *John/Taupin 3:09 (B)*
MCA 40421 (US). Released June 23, 1975
Producer: Gus Dudgeon
Studio: Caribou Ranch, Colorado, USA
Recorded: June/July 1974

23 **ISLAND GIRL** *John/Taupin 3:46 (A)*
SUGAR ON THE FLOOR *Kiki Dee 4:31 (B)*
MCA 40461 (US). Released September 29, 1975
Producer: Gus Dudgeon
Studio: Caribou Ranch, Colorado, USA
Recorded: July 1975

24 **I FEEL LIKE A BULLET (IN THE GUN OF
ROBERT FORD)** *John/Taupin 5:30 (A)*
GROW SOME FUNK OF YOUR OWN
John/Taupin/Johnstone 4:45 (B)
MCA 40505 (US). Released January 12, 1976
Producer: Gus Dudgeon
Studio: Caribou Ranch, Colorado, USA
Recorded: July 1975

25 **DON'T GO BREAKING MY HEART**
*Orson/Blanche 4:23 (A)**
SNOW QUEEN *John/Taupin/Johnstone/*
Dee/Nutter 5:54 (B)
MCA Rocket 40585 (US). Released June 21, 1976
Producer: Gus Dudgeon
Studio: Eastern Sound, Toronto
Recorded: March 1976
*Duet with Kiki Dee

26 **SORRY SEEMS TO BE THE HARDEST WORD**
John/Taupin 3:43 (A)
SHOULDER HOLSTER *John/Taupin 5:05 (B)*
MCA/Rocket 40645 (US).
Released November 1, 1976
Producer: Gus Dudgeon
Studio: Eastern Sound, Toronto
Recorded: March 1976

27 **BITE YOUR LIP (GET UP & DANCE)**
John/Taupin 3:37 (A)
CHAMELEON *John/Taupin 5:25 (B)*
MCA/Rocket 40677 (US). Released January 31, 1977
Producer: Gus Dudgeon
Studio: Eastern Sound, Toronto
Recorded: March 1976

28 **EGO** *John/Taupin 3:57 (A)*
FLINTSTONE BOY *John/   4:07 (B)*
MCA 40892 (US). Released March 1978
Producer: Elton John/Clive Franks
Studio: The Mill at Cookham, Berkshire
Recorded: January - March 1978

29 **SONG FOR GUY** *John 5:01 (A)*
LOVESICK *John/Taupin 3:55 (B)*
MCA 40993 (US). Released March 1979
Producer: Elton John/Clive Franks
Studio: The Mill at Cookham, Berkshire
Recorded: *(A)(B)* January 1978

30 **MAMA CAN'T BUY YOU LOVE** *L. Bell/*
   C. James 4:03 (A)
   THREE-WAY LOVE AFFAIR *L. Bell/C. James 5:31 (B)*
   MCA 41042 (US) 7″ disc 45 rpm. Released June 1979
   Producer: Thom Bell
   Studio: Sigma Sound Studios, Philadelphia
   Kay Smith Studio, Seattle
   Recorded: October 1977

31 **MAMA CAN'T BUY YOU LOVE** *L. Bell/*
   C. James 4:03 (A)
   THREE WAY LOVE AFFAIR *L. Bell/C. James 5:31 (B)*
   ARE YOU READY FOR LOVE *L. Bell/T. Bell*
   C. James 8:31 (C)
   MCA 13921 (US) 12″ disc. Released June 1979
   Producer: Thom Bell
   Studio: Kay Smith Studio, Seattle
   Sigma and Sound Studios, Philadelphia
   Recorded: October 1977

32 **VICTIM OF LOVE** *Bellotte/Le Vay/Rix 3:18 (A)*
   STRANGERS *John/Osborne 4:40 (B)*
   MCA 41126 (US). Released September 1979
   Producer: Pete Bellotte *(A)* Elton John/
   Clive Franks *(B)*
   Studio: Musicland, Munich, *(A)* The Mill at Cookham,
   Berkshire *(B)*
   Recorded: August 1979 *(A)* March 1978 *(B)*

33 **PART-TIME LOVE** *John/Osborne 3:12 (A)*
   I CRY AT NIGHT *John/Taupin 3:10 (B)*
   MCA 40973 (US). Released November 1979
   Producer: Elton John/Clive Franks
   Studio: The Mill at Cookham, Berkshire
   Recorded: March 1978

34 **JOHNNY B. GOODE** *Berry 3:22 (A)*
   GEORGIA *John/Osborne 4:41 (B)*
   MCA 41159 (US). Released December 1979
   Producer: Pete Bellotte *(A)* Elton John/
   Clive Franks *(B)*
   Studio: Musicland, Munich; Rusk Sound,
   Hollywood *(A)* The Mill at Cookham, Berkshire *(B)*
   Recorded: August 1979 *(A)* March 1978 *(B)*

35 **LITTLE JEANNIE** *John/Osborne 5:18 (A)*
   CONQUER THE SUN *John/Osborne 4:16 (B)*
   MCA 41236 (US). Released May 17, 1980
   Producer: Elton John/Clive Franks
   Studio: Superbear Studios, Nice
   Recorded: August 1979

36 **DON'T YA WANNA PLAY THIS GAME
   NO MORE?** *John/Robinson 4:44 (A)*
   CARTIER *Dinah Card/Carte Blanche 0:53 (B)*
   WHITE MAN DANGER *John/Taupin 5:25 (C)*
   MCA 41293 (US). Released August 1980
   Producer: Elton John/Clive Franks
   Studio: Superbear Studios, Nice, France *(A, C)*
   Recorded: August 1979 *(A)* August 1979 *(C)*

37 **NOBODY WINS** *John/Osborne*
   FOOLS IN FASHION *John/Taupin*
   Geffen GEF 49722 (US). Released May 6, 1981
   Producer: Chris Thomas *(A)*
   Studio: Sunset Sound, Los Angeles
   Recorded: August 1979 to March 1980

BOOTLEGS

The publishers & the author have absolutely no knowledge regarding the buying and selling of bootlegs. This listing is a discography *not* a catalogue.

On the whole, bootlegs of Elton John's music are not available in such abundance, or as easy to find, as many other artists i.e. Dylan, The Beatles, The Stones etc. although it would hardly be argued that he has not been one of, if not the, most successful recording stars of the seventies.

Possibly the most interesting of these releases is the "Studio Bootleg" (the only one known to be in existence) which consists of studio piano demos. It is called "I Get A Little Bit Lonely" and appeared in the US in early 1976. Rumours abounded regarding the source of the recordings, but there is little doubt that it was the cause of much aggravation to Elton's US record company MCA and it wasn't long before the bootleggers were halted in their tracks. Apparently very few copies actually hit the streets, and it is doubtful if a great number reached England as it was pressed in America; thus it has become the rarest bootleg put out on Elton.

All other bootleg releases are recordings of Elton's concert appearances and vary in quality. Next to the title in this section a number appears which denotes a grading of quality per record. These start at (1) which is virtually unplayable climbing to (10) which is excellent stereo/mono. However good though, a bootleg can never be as good as the official product.

Bootlegs are of course illegal, and as such are a continual thorn in the side of the record companies. From a record collector's point of view, once they have bought all the official products, including singles released from albums, then they will also buy the bootlegs if and when they are available and are not covered by an official release. If a record company does not put, say, "Live At Joe's" out on the market and a bootlegger does, can that record company claim that they are losing revenue? Moot point.

Nearly all bootlegs are limited runs of 1,000 or 2,000, sometimes even less when they are pressed locally. 'Counterfeits' and 'Pirates' are in an altogether different category.

It has been known for certain artists to turn a blind eye to bootlegs of their concerts, and even on occasions to encourage them. They tend to feel that only true fans buy them. An example of this is when Bruce Springsteen told his audience to "Get your tapes rolling, this is going to be a good one". The only way to stop their sales is to stop them from being manufactured. This is proving a big task for those concerned.

1 **ALL ACROSS THE HAVENS** (9)
TAKRL 1946 US Pressing
Recorded: Hammersmith Odeon, London
December 24, 1974.
PA recording excellent stereo

Side One:
1. Funeral For a Friend *11:06*
2. Love Lies Bleeding
3. Candle In the Wind *3:40*
4. Grimsby *3:20*
5. Crocodile Rock *3:35*
Side Two:
6. Goodbye Yellow Brick Road *3:04*
7. Grey Seal *5:08*
8. Don't Let The Sun Go Down On Me *5:30*
9. Saturday Night's Alright for Fighting *8:20*
10. Your Song *3.10*
Note: Probably the best of all Elton's bootlegs for
quality. This LP is Part 2 of a Double Album called
"Pink Eyed In Paradise".
Band line up: Elton, Dee Murray, Nigel Olsson,
Davey Johnstone, Ray Cooper

2 **ALL THE YOUNG GIRLS LOVE ALICE** (7)
HHEJ1 US Pressing
Recorded: Hollywood Bowl, California
September 7, 1973. Audience recording Stereo/Mono

Side One
1. Honky Cat 5:35
2. Goodbye Yellow Brick Road 2:50
3. Rocket Man 3:55
4. All The Young Girls Love Alice 4:30
5. Daniel 3:30
Side Two:
6. Madman Across the Water 11:00
7. Teacher I Need You 4:10
8. Crocodile Rock 3:20
Band line up: Elton, Nigel Olsson, Dee Murray,
Davey Johnstone, Clive Franks on 'Crocodile Rock' only.

3 APPLE PIE (6)
HHCER 105 US Pressing
Recorded: Scope Auditorium, Norfolk, Virginia
November 13, 1972
Side One:
1. Tiny Dancer 5:45
2. Daniel 3:30
3. Suzie (Dramas) 3:10
4. Your Song 3:50
5. Levon 6:30
Side Two:
6. Can I Put You On 8:15
7. Goodbye Yellow Brick Road* 2:50
8. Mona Lisas and Mad Hatters 4:30
9. Honky Cat 3:25
Note: *Taken from Hollywood Bowl Concert 1973
Band line up: Elton, Dee Murray, Nigel Olsson
Note: Davey Johnstone was in the band at this time but
didn't appear due to illness

4 B – B – B – BENNY (3)
GLC 413 UK Pressing by Great Live Concerts
Recorded: Hammersmith Odeon, London
Saturday December 22, 1973 Stereo/Double Album/Live
Side One:
1. Funeral For a Friend 10:51
2. Love Lies Bleeding

3. Candle In the Wind *3:36*
4. A Cat Named 'Hercules' *8:20*
Side Two:
5. Rocket Man *4:30*
6. Bennie & The Jets *5:40*
7. Daniel *3:35*
8. This Song Has No Title *2:18*
9. Honky Cat *6:40*

(Front)

(Back)

Side Three:
10. Goodbye Yellow Brick Road *3:00*
11. Ballad of Danny Bailey, 1909-34, The *5:30*
12. Elderberry Wine *5:20*
13. Rudolph the Red Nosed Reindeer
14. I've Seen That Movie Too *5:30*
Side Four:
15. All The Young Girls Love Alice *6:50*
16. Crocodile Rock *3:30*
17. Your Song *3:40*
18. Saturday Night's Alright for Fighting *7:40*
Band line up: Elton, Dee Murray, Nigel Olsson, Davey
Johnstone, Ray Cooper, Clive Franks on 'Crocodile
Rock'.

5 **THE BITCH IS BACK** (9)
WPLJ1 US Pressing Stereo
Recorded: Same as the official LP 'Caribou'
Studio Stereo

Side One:
1. The Bitch is Back *3:42*
2. Pinky *3:53*
3. Grimsby *3:47*
4. Dixie Lily *2:48*
5. Solar Prestige A Gammon *2:50*
6. You're So Static *4:49*
Side Two:
7. I've Seen the Saucers *4:45*
8. Stinker *5:16*
9. Don't Let the Sun Go Down On Me *5:33*
10. Ticking *7:43*
Note: This album apparently appeared on the streets in the USA before 'Caribou'. The tapes were supposedly borrowed without anybody knowing about it. It is also rumoured that the 'Caribou' LP was to be called 'The Bitch is Back'.

6 **BITCHIN IN LA** (7)
P1113 US Pressing
Recorded: The Forum, Los Angeles October 5, 1974 same as 'Elton In Disguise With Glasses'. Audience recording stereo live
See "Elton In Disguise With Glasses"
Band line up: Elton, Dee Murray, Nigel Olsson, Ray Cooper, Davey Johnstone, The Muscle Shoals Horns

7 **CLOSET KEEPERS** (8)
TAKRL 1380 US Pressing by The Amazing Kornyphone Record Label
Recorded: The Forum, Inglewood, California. October 5, 1974 Stereo Live
Side One:
1. Grimsby *3:30*
2. Rocket Man *3:40*
3. Take Me To The Pilot *5:55*
4. Bennie & The Jets *5:20*
5. Grey Seal *4:40*
Side Two:
6. Daniel *3:30*

7. You're So Static *4:10*
8. Lucy In The Sky With Diamonds *5:30*
9. Don't Let The Sun Go Down On Me *5:20*
10. Honky Cat *6:00*
Band line up: Elton, Dee Murray, Nigel Olsson, Davey Johnstone, Ray Cooper, The Muscle Shoals Horns.

8 **COUNTRY COMFORT** (7)
   MR 1369 US pressing by Phonygraf
   Recorded: Santa Monica, Los Angeles, California
   November 15, 1970 Stereo/Mono Live
   Side One:
   1. Your Song *3:50*
   2. Take Me To The Pilot *6:30*
   3. Country Comfort *4:55*
   4. 60 Years On *6:50*
   5. Border Song *3:20*
   Side Two:
   6. Honky Tonk Woman *4:00*
   7. Burn Down the Mission *7:00*
   8. Give Peace a Chance/Finis/Medley Get Back *13:00*
   Band line up: Elton, Dee Murray, Nigel Olsson

9 **ELTON IN DISGUISE WITH GLASSES** (8)
   P1113 US Pressing by Phonygraf
   Recorded: The Forum, Inglewood, California October 5,
   1974 Stereo/Mono/Live

Side One:
1. Grimsby *3:30*
2. Rocket Man *3:40*
3. Take Me to the Pilot *5:55*
4. Bennie & The Jets *5:20*
5. Grey Seal *4:40*
Side Two:
6. Daniel *3:30*
7. You're So Static *4:10*
8. Lucy In the Sky with Diamonds *5:30*
9. Don't Let the Sun Go Down On Me *5:20*
10. Honky Cat *6:00*
Notes: This is a much better pressing than the 'Bitchin In LA' Bootleg
Band line up: Elton, Dee Murray, Nigel Olsson, Davey Johnstone, Ray Cooper, The Muscle Shoals Horns

(Alternative)

10 **ELTON AT ANAHEIM** (7)
70010 US Pressing by Rubber Dubber
Recorded: Anaheim Convention Centre, California
December 4, 1970 Stereo/Live
Side One:
1. Your Song *4:05*
2. This is My Life (Bad Side of the Moon) *4:10*
3. Can I Put You On *7:30*
4. Honky Tonk Woman *4:00*
Side Two:
5. Burn Down the Mission
6. Get Back *19:00*
7. My Baby Left Me
Note: This LP was coupled with a Leon Russell LP also live from Anaheim – making a double LP
Band line up: Elton, Dee Murray, Nigel Olsson

11 **ELDERBERRY WINE** (8)
B.2047/8 US Pressing by Berkely
Recorded: Hammersmith Odeon, London December 22, 1973 – same as "Untitled" Stereo Double Album
See "Untitled" for Track Listing
Band line up: Elton, Dee Murray, Nigel Olsson, Davey Johnstone, Ray Cooper, Clive Franks on 'Crocodile Rock'

12 **THE ELTON JOHN STORY** (9)
Footprint Canadian Pressing by A S & S Production
Recorded: CJOM FM Windsor, Ontario
Broadcast of E J Story narrated by Roger Scott
July 28/29, 1973 Stereo
Notes: 4 LP Set. Contains interviews, early demo
segments, studio tracks. 4 hours long – over 40 songs
featured.
*Although Roger Scott appears on this LP set he has
nothing whatsoever to do with the manufacture of this
album.

13 **THE ELTON JOHN STORY (SINGLE 45)** (9)
Footprint T57397 US Pressing by Footprint
Syndications
Recorded: CJOM FM Windsor, Ontario
Taken from the 4 LP set Scott Sinclair Productions
Notes: Various cuts from Official Albums up to 1973
Sample 45 Promoting Album Set. Features 'Your Song'
Demo 5:50

14 **GET DOWN WITH LITTLE RICHARD**
REDITA LP 114 Dutch Pressing
Recorded: Various. Little Richard Tracks 60's onwards
Side One:
Track (1) Get Down With 3:00
Track (2) Rose Marie 2:40
Note: There are 17 tracks on this album – all by Little
Richard. LP states that the above tracks have backing by
Bluesologie. From 1966 – whether this is the Bluesology
that Elton was with is not known. The tracks were
recorded at EMI's Croydon Studios.

15 **A GUITAR'S ALRIGHT JOHN BUT YOU'LL
NEVER EARN YOUR LIVING BY IT** (8)
R6015 German Pressing by Audifon
Recorded: This is a John Lennon Bootleg. Side 1 is taken
from Madison Square Garden, New York, November 28,
1974 Stereo/Live
Side One:
1. Whatever Gets You Through the Night 3:05

2. Lucy In the Sky with Diamonds *5:40*
3. I Saw Her Standing There *3:05*
Side Two:
4. Slippin' and Slidin' *2:20*
5. Stand By Me *3:45*
6. Oh My Love *2:46*
7. Lady Marmalade *0.50*
8. Working Class Hero *2:22*

A guitar's all right John
but you'll never earn your living by it.

Notes: Band line up for Side 1: Elton, John Lennon,
Davey Johnstone, Dee Murray, Nigel Olsson, Ray
Cooper, Muscle Shoals Horns.
Sadly this was John Lennon's last concert. He joined
Elton on stage for three songs on Side 1.
This disc was pressed as a ten-inch on five different
colours. Until 1981 these 3 tracks were available only on
this bootleg. "Whatever Gets You Through the Night"
was available on another John Lennon bootleg called
"Plop Plop Fizz Fizz" HAR 170 but the quality was
terrible.
"I Saw Her Standing There" was the only track officially
available – on the 'B' side on Elton's single 'Philadelphia
Freedom', until John Lennon's death.

16 **GULLIVER'S GONE** (9)
FIW US Pressing
Recorded: Direct Pirate of "Empty Sky" Official Release
Studio Stereo
Same as "Empty Sky" Official Release
Notes: This pirate was available in the US for some time
due to the fact that the 'Empty Sky' LP was only
available on import.
MCA eventually released the album in 1975. The pirate
obviously affected sales of the genuine release.

17 **HECHO EN MEXICO** (7)
IMP EJ3 US Pressing by Idel Mind
Recorded: The San Diego Sports Arena, California
August 29, 1975 Stereo/Live
Side One:
1. Meal Ticket (Gotta Get A) *8:20*
2. Island Girl *3:35*

3. Philadelphia Freedom *5:25*
4. Better Off Dead *2:40*
5. Harmony *2:50*
Side Two:
6. Captain Fantastic & The Brown Dirt Cowboy *5:45*
7. Someone Saved My Life Tonight *7:15*
8. Don't Let the Sun Go Down On Me *5:40*

Band line up: Elton, Davey Johnstone, Ray Cooper,
James Newton-Howard, Caleb Quaye, Roger Pope,
Kenny Passerelli

18 **ISLAND GIRLS** (7)
CBM US Pressing by Contraband Music
Recorded: Sports Arena, San Diego, California
Same as "Hecho En Mexico" Stereo
See "Hecho En Mexico"
Band line up: Elton, Davey Johnstone, Ray Cooper,
James Newton-Howard, Caleb Quaye, Roger Pope,
Kenny Passerelli

19 **I GET A LITTLE BIT LONELY** (9)
APPY 1/2 US Pressing by Appy Records
Recorded: DJM Studio Demos Circa 1968/69/70
Stereo/Mono/Studio
Side One:
1. I Get A Little Bit Lonely* *2:18*
2. The Flowers Will Never Die* *2:53*

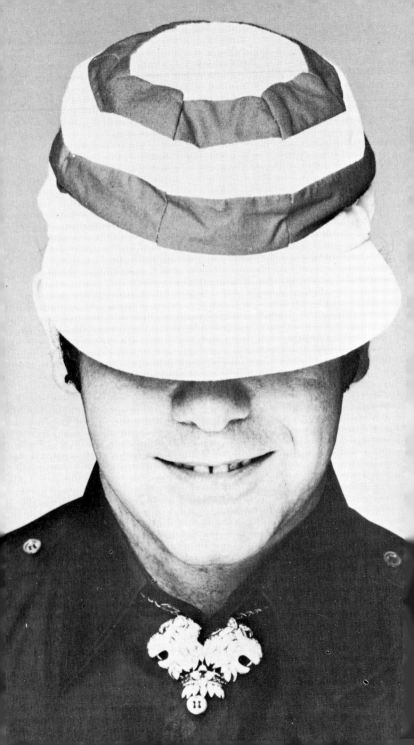

3. Rock Me When He's Gone* *4:09*
4. Tartan Coloured Lady *3:55*
5. I've Been Loving You*** *3.01*
6. Sitting Doing Nothing *2:36*
7. Sing Me No Sad Songs *2:42*
Side Two:
8. I Love You & That's All That Matters *3:35*
9. The Tide Will Turn for Rebecca* *2:58*
10. A Dandelion Dies in the Wind *3:15*
11. Hourglass *3:00*
12. Baby I Miss You *3:36*
13. Reminds Me Of You *2:53*
14. When the First Tear Shows* *3:05*
Notes: This bootleg is undoubtedly the rarest and most collectable of all Elton's Bootlegs. A mixture of mixed and unmixed studio demos, none of which has been released by Elton with the exception of "I've Been Loving You"***
Tracks marked * have been released by other artists.

20 **JUST LIKE STRANGE RAIN** (9)
TAKRL 1974 US Pressing by the Amazing Kornyphone Label
Recorded: Hammersmith Odeon, London
December 24, 1974 Stereo Live
Side One:
1. Rocket Man *4:30*
2. High Flying Bird *3:50*
3. Burn Down the Mission *10:15*
4. The Bitch is Back *3:30*
Side Two:
5. Daniel *3:35*
6. Bennie & The Jets *4:30*
7. Lucy In the Sky with Diamonds *5:30*
8. I Saw Her Standing There *2:50*
9. Honky Cat *6:40*
Notes: This LP is Part I of "Pink Eyed In Paradise" "All Across The Havens" is Part II
Band line up: Elton, Dee Murray, Nigel Olsson, Davey Johnstone, Ray Cooper

21 **KNOCKING 'EM DEAD ALIVE" (9)**
KR 2006 US Pressing by Kustom Records
Recorded: FM Recording of Live concert put out by
WABC New York November 17, 1970 – Stereo – Double
Album

Side One:
1. I Need You to Turn To *2:20*
2. Your Song *3:40*
3. Far Side of the Moon *4:25*
4. Country Comfort *4:55*
Side Two:
5. Can I Put You Off (On) *6:20*
6. Border Song *4:00*
7. Sixty Years On *8:05*
Side Three:
8. Indian Sunset *7:15*
9. Honky Tonk Woman *4:09*
10. Amoreena *4:45*
11. Take me to the Pilot *6:43*
Side Four:
12. Burn Down the Mission *18:00*
13. Medley (Inc. 'Get Back')
14. My Baby Left Me
15. My Father's Gun *5:05*
Notes: This Bootleg forced DJM/MCA/UNI to release
the "17.11.70" official LP
Band line up: Elton, Dee Murray, Nigel Olsson

22 **LIVE IN LONDON (7)**
STR 001 UK Pressing by 'The Strait Record Co'
Recorded: 'Crystal Palace' Garden Party, London
Saturday July 31, 1971 Stereo Live
Side One:
1. Skyline Pigeon *3:10*
2. Rock Me When He's Gone *3:15*
3. I Need You To Turn To *2:05*
4. Tiny Dancer *6:07*
5. Love Song *3:20*
Side Two:
6. Razor Face *3:20*

7. Indian Sunset *6:00*
8. Whole Lotta Shakin' *6:40*

Note: This is another of Elton's rare bootlegs.
Apparently all but a few copies of this were destroyed
soon after pressing.
Band line up: Elton, Dee, Nigel

23 **LIVE IN AUSTRALIA** (7)
EJI Australian Pressing by unknown
Recorded: Randwick Racetrack, Australia March 14,
1974 Stereo/Live
Side One:
1. Funeral For a Friend
2. Love Lies Bleeding *11.00*
3. Candle in the Wind *3:35*
4. Goodbye Yellow Brick Road *3:00*
Side Two:
5. Bennie & The Jets *4:50*
6. Honky Cat *5:30*
7. Your Song *3:50*
Band line up: Elton, Dee Murray, Nigel Olsson, Davey
Johnstone, Ray Cooper

24 **LIVE AT THE STADIUM** (6)
WEM 1/2 US Pressing by unknown
Recorded: Wembley Stadium, London Saturday June 21,
1975 Stereo/Live

Side One:
1. Captain Fantastic & The Brown Dirt Cowboy *5:45*
2. Meal Ticket (Gotta Get A) *7:30*
3. Better Off Dead *2:35*
4. Tell Me When the Whistle Blows *4:15*
Side 2
5. Someone Saved My Life Tonight *7:00*
6. We all Fall in Love Some Time *4:25*
7. Curtains *6:10*
Band line up: Elton, Kenny Passerelli, James Newton-Howard, Ray Cooper, Davey Johnstone, Caleb Quaye, Roger Pope, Jeff (Skunk) Baxter appeared as guest for this concert.

25 **LUCY IN THE SKY** (7)
CBM EJ US Pressing by Contraband Music
Recorded: The Forum Inglewood, California October 5, 1974 Stereo/Mono Live
Same as "Elton in Disguise with Glasses"
Band line up: Elton, Nigel Olsson, Dee Murray, Ray Cooper

26 **LIVE E JAY** (9)
2006 US Pressing
Recorded: WABC New York FM Recording November 17, 1970
Same as "Knocking 'Em Dead Alive" Stereo/Live
See "Knocking 'Em Dead Alive"
Band line up: Elton, Dee Murray, Nigel Olsson

27 **LIVE EJ** (6)
CBM US Pressing by Contraband Music
Recorded: Scope Auditorium, Norfolk, Virginia
Same LP as "Apple Pie" Mono/Live
See "Apple Pie" Bootleg
Note: This is a poor pressing by 'Contraband'

28 **MORE ROCK FROM ELTON** (8)
TMQ 73039 US Pressing by Trademark of Quality
Recorded: "The Swing Auditorium" San Bernadino, California November 1970 Audience Stereo/Live

Cover says recorded Dec 71
Side One:
1. Your Song *3:55*
2. Bad Side of The Moon *4:24*
3. Border Song *3:20*
4. Can I Put You On *7:20*
Side Two:
5. Country Comfort *4:30*
6. 60 Years On *7:00*
7. Honky Tonk Woman *4:00*

Note: Originals of this album were pressed on green
vinyl. Idle Mind copied this LP and put it out under their
own label.
Band line up: Elton, Dee Murray, Nigel Olsson

29 "OL' PINK EYES IS BACK" (8)
WRMB 331 US Pressing by Wizard Records
Recorded: BBC Broadcast from Hammersmith Odeon,
London December 24, 1974 Mono/Live
Side One:
1. Funeral For a Friend
2. Love Lies Bleeding *11:06*
3. Candle In The Wind *3:40*
4. Grimsby *3:20*
Side Two:
5. Goodbye Yellow Brick Road *3:04*
6. Grey Seal *5:08*
7. Don't Let The Sun Go Down On Me *5:30*

8. Saturday Night's Alright for Fighting *8:20*
Side Three:
9. Rocket Man *4:30*
10. High Flying Bird *3:50*
11. Burn Down the Mission *10:15*
12. The Bitch is Back *3:30*
Side Four:
13. Daniel *3:35*
14. Bennie & The Jets *4:30*
15. Lucy In the Sky With Diamonds *5:30*
16. I Saw Her Standing There *2:50*
17. Honky Cat *6:40*
Band line up: Elton, Dee Murray, Nigel Olsson, Ray
Cooper, Davey Johnstone, Muscle Shoals Horns.

30 **OPENING NIGHT** (8)
US Pressing by unknown
Recorded: Los Angeles Universal Amphitheatre
September 26, 1979 Stereo/Live
Side One:
1. I Heard It Through the Grapevine *6:10*
2. I Feel Like a Bullet (In the Gun of Robert Ford) *3:20*
3. Benny & The Jets *9:30*
Side Two:
4. Tonight *7:05*
5. Better Off Dead *2:35*
6. Idol *3:45*
7. I Think I'm Gonna Kill Myself *3:10*
Notes: This is a Bootleg of Elton's 'Single Man' tour with
Ray Cooper

(Alternative)

31 **ROCK AND ROLL MADONNA** (8)
TAKRL 1907 US Pressing by The Amazing Kornyphone
Label
Recorded: *These tracks are direct from officially
released Elton Tracks and from the "Knocking 'Em
Dead Alive" Album Stereo/Mono/Studio/Live
Side One:
1. Bad Side of the Moon* *2:56*
2. Lady Samantha* *3:01*

3. It's Me That You Need* *3.50*
4. Border Song *4:25*
5. Into the Old Man's Shoes* *3:58*
6. Country Comfort *5:37*
7. Screw You* *4:45*
Side Two:
8. I Need You To Turn To *2:32*
9. Rock & Roll Madonna* *4:17*
10. Grey Seal* *3:30*
11. Amoreena *4:51*
12. Jack Rabbit* *1:50*
13. Step Into Xmas* *4:30*
14. Ho! Ho! Ho! Who'd Be A Turkey at Xmas* *4:10*
15. Whenever You're Ready, We'll Go
Steady Again* *2:50*
Notes: This Bootleg bears similarity to the official Tape
Only compilation 'Lady Samantha' released in the UK
only.
Tracks Marked * are live from the 'Knockin 'Em Dead
Alive' album
Berkely Records copied this album. Cover is deluxe. A
much better press Cat. No.2037

32 "RADIOCORD" (7)
CBM 354000 US Pressing by Contraband Music
Recorded: WABC New York NY FM Broadcast.
November 17, 1970 Stereo/Live.
Side One:
1. Indian Sunset *7:15*
2. My Father's Gun *5:10*
3. Honky Tonk Woman *4:00*
4. Can I Put You On *6:15*
Side Two
5. Far Side Of The Moon *4:25*
6. Burn Down The Mission *18.16*
7. Get Back
8. My Baby Left Me
Note: A later reissue of this LP had a new hard type
cover pressed on blue vinyl.
Band line up: Elton, Dee Murray, Nigel Olsson

33 **"ROCK OF THE EASTIES"** (7)
TKRWM 1372 US Pressing by Trade Mark of Quality
Released Los Angeles,October 1974 Stereo/Mono Live
Side One:
1. Daniel *3:30*
2. You're So Static *4:10*
3. Lucy In The Sky With Diamonds *5:30*
4. Don't Let The Sun Go Down On Me *5:20*
5. Honky Cat *6:00*
Side Two:
5. Grimsby *3:30*
6. Rocket Man *3:40*
7. Take Me To The Pilot *5:55*
8. Bennie & The Jets *5:20*
9. Grey Seal *4:40*
Band line up: Elton, Dee Murray, Nigel Olsson, Davey
Johnstone, Muscle Shoals Horn, Ray Cooper.

34 **"SCOPE 72"** (7)
HHLER 105 US Pressing by Hiway HI.
Recorded: Scope Auditorium, Norfolk, Virginia,
November 1972 same as "Apple Pie" Live/Mono.
Side One:
1. Tiny Dancer *5:43*
2. Daniel *3:26*
3. Susie (Dramas) *3:10*
4. Your Song *3:45*
5. Levon *6:25*
Side Two:
6. Can I Put You On *8:15*
7. Goodbye Yellow Brick Road* *2:55*
8. Mona Lisas & Mad Hatters *4:30*
9. Honky Cat *3:25*
*Taken from "Hollywood Bowl Concert"
Band line up: Elton, Nigel Olsson, Dee Murray.

35 **"SNOOKEROO/"HONEY MAN"** (Single 45)
(10)/(9)
Disc label has UNI 1161R
"Snookeroo" – Piano Demo by Elton
"Honey Man" – with Cat Stevens – Recorded at PYE
Studios, London
Side One:
Snookeroo *3:15* Stereo
Side Two:
Honey Man *2:55* Mono
Notes: Taken from a test pressing. Snookeroo was
recorded by Ringo Starr for his LP "Goodnight Vienna.
Elton played piano on this track. Written by Elton
John/Bernie Taupin.
Honey Man – Elton and Cat Stevens recorded this track
in 1971. Cat Stevens plays piano. Record company
politics prevented the official release. Written by

Cat Stevens/Ken Cumberbach.
The song was eventually released by
Brotherly Love and Sweet Salvation.

36 "SUPERSTAR LIVE (7)

EJL 501 UK Pressing by Unknown
Recorded: Cuts taken from various Live Concerts in
1970 – a kind of Bootleg "Greatest Hits" Stereo/Mono
Side One:
1. I Need You To Turn To *2:30*
2. Your Song *3:50*
3. Bad Side Of The Moon *4:20*
4. Country Comfort *4:55*
Side Two:
5. Border Song *4:00*
6. 60 Years On *7:05*
7. Honky Tonk Woman *4:00*
8. Amarina (their spelling) *5:45*
Band line up: Elton, Dee Murray, Nigel Olsson.

37 "UNTITLED" AKA "NO TITLE" (9)

TAKRL 2927 US Pressing by the Amazing Kornyphone
Record Label
Recorded: BBC FM Broadcast from Hammersmith
Odeon, London. December 22nd 1973 Stereo/Live
Side One:
1. Funeral For A Friend *10:57*
2. Love Lies Bleeding .

3. Candle In The Wind *3:37*
4. A Cat Named Hercules *8:23*
Side Two:
5. Rocket Man *4:31*
6. Bennie & The Jets *5:40*
7. Daniel *3:35*
8. This Song Has No Title *2:18*
9. Honky Cat *6:48*
Side Three:
10. Goodbye Yellow Brick Road *2:56*
11. Ballad of Danny Bailey *5:53*
12. Elderberry Wine *5:15*
13. I've Seen That Movie Too *5:30*
Side Four:
14. All The Young Girls Love Alice *6:53*
15. Crocodile Rock *3:26*
16. Your Song *3:40*
17. Saturday Night's Alright For Fighting *7:40*
Notes: Also known as "No Title"
Band line up: Elton, Ray Cooper, Nigel Olsson, Dee Murra
Davey Johnstone, Clive Franks on 'Crocodile Rock'.

38 "VERY ALIVE" (8)
US Pressing by Keylo Records
Recorded: This album is taken from the FM Broadcast
17.11.70 in New York Stereo/Live
Side One:
1. Bad Side Of The Moon *4:25*
2. Can I Put You On *6:15*
3. Indian Sunset *7:15*
4. Honky Tonk Woman *4:00*
Side Two:
5. Burn Down The Mission *19:00*
6. My Baby Left Me
7. Get Back
8. My Father's Gun *5:05*
Band line up: Elton, Nigel Olsson, Dee Murray

39 "WEST OF THE ROCKIES" (8)
IMP 1104 US Pressing by Impossible Records

Recorded: Side 1 – Dodger Stadium, Los Angeles,
October 25, 1975. Side 2 – San Diego, California,
August 29, 1975 Stereo/Live
Side One:
1. Your Song *3:50*
2. Lucy In The Sky With Diamonds *5:25*
3. I Saw Her Standing There *2:30*
4. Island Girl *3:30*
5. Harmony *2:50*
6. Pinball Wizard *6:05*
Side Two:
7. Captain Fantastic & The Brown Dirt Cowboy *5:45*
8. Someone Saved My Life Tonight *7:15*
9. Don't Let The Sun Go Down On Me *3:40*
Band line up: Elton, Davey Johnstone, Kenny Passerelli,
Ray Cooper, Roger Pope, Caleb Quaye, James Newton-
Howard.

A Cat Named Hercules, 92
A Dandelion Dies In The Wind, 83
All Across The Havens, 8,62
All The Nasties, 35
All The Young Girls Love Alice,
   39,74,75,92
Amoreena, 33,84,89,91
Amy, 37
Are You Ready For Love, 20,21,67

Baby I Miss You, 83
Bad Side Of The Moon, 9,33,57,
   62,87,88,91,92
Ballad Of A Well-Known Gun, 32
Ballad Of Danny Bailey (1909-34) –
   The, 39,55,75,92
Bennie & The Jets, 13,15,20,38,
   44,47,48,54,58,64,75,76,78,
   83,85,88,90,92
Better Off Dead, 41,48, 81,86,88
Between Seventeen And Twenty, 45
Big Dipper, 49
Billy Bones And The White Bird, 44
Bitch Is Back – The 13,19,39,47,53,
   58,64,76,83,88
Bite Your Lip (Get Up And Dance),
   16,17,45,66
Bitter Fingers, 41
Blues For My Baby & Me, 38,54
Boogie Pilgrim, 45
Border Song, 9,18,32,40,44,53,57,
   62,77,84,87,89,91
Born Bad, 55
Breaking Down The Barriers, 59
Burn Down The Mission, 33,48,53,
   77,78,83,84,88,89,92

Cage – The, 32,53
Cage The Songbird, 45
Candle In The Wind, 13,19,38,40,
   48,54,57,73,75,85,87,92
Can I Put You On, 33;34,74,78,
   84,87,89,90,92
Can't Get Over Getting Over
   Losing You, 24
Captain Fantastic & The Brown
   Dirt Cowboy, 41,55,81,86,93
Carla, 59
Cartier, 23,70
Chameleon, 16,45,66
Chasing The Crown, 56
Chicago (Kiki Dee), 16,17
Chloe, 59
Cold Highway, 13,64
Come Back Baby, 8
Come Down In Time, 32
Conquer The Sun, 22,67
Country Comfort, 18,32,53,77,84,
   87,89,91
Crazy Water, 16,45
Crocodile Rock, 10,18,38,40,44,
   53,58,63,73,74,75,92
Curtains, 17,41,55,86

Dan Dare (Pilot Of The Future),
   41,48
Daniel, 10,18,38,40,54,57,58,63,
   74,75,76,78,83,88,90,92

Dear God, 23,56
Dirty Little Girl, 39
Dixie Lily, 39,76
Don't Go Breaking My Heart, 15,
   47,57,58,66
Don't Let The Sun Go Down
   On Me, 13,19,39,40,48,54,57,
   58,64,73,76,77,78,81,87,90,93
Don't Ya Wanna Play This Game
   No More (Sartorial Eloquence), 70

Ego, 17,66
Elderberry Wine, 10,38,48,53,
   63,75,92
Elton's Song, 59
Empty Sky, 31,52
Etude, 59
Every Day (I Have The Blues), 8

Fanfare, 59
Far Side Of The Moon
   (Bad Side Of The Moon), 84,89
Fascist Faces, 59
Feed Me, 44
First Episode At Hienton, 32
Flintstone Boy, 17, 66
Flowers Will Never Die, The, 81
Fools In Fashion, 24, 70
Fox, The, 59
Friends, 9,34,53,57,63
From Denver To L.A., 62
Funeral For A Friend, 17,38,44,
   54,73,74,85,87,91

Georgia, 52,67
Get Back, 33,78,89,92
Give Me The Love, 56
Give Peace A Chance, 77
Goaldigger Song, 16
Goodbye, 9,35,63
Goodbye Yellow Brick Road, 13,
   19,38,40,54,57,58,64,73,74,75,
   85,87,90,92
Greatest Discovery, The, 32,54
Grey Seal, 9,38,48,53,57,73,76,
   78,87,89,90
Grimsby, 39,73,76,78,87,90
Grow Some Funk Of Your Own,
   15,19,41,47,53,65
Gulliver, 31

Hard Luck Story, 44
Harmony, 15,23,39,54,57,
   64,81,93
Have Mercy On The Criminal, 38
Hay-Chewed, 31
Heart In The Right Place, 59
Hercules, 37,75
Heels Of The Wind, 59
Here's To The Next Time, 8
High Flying Bird, 38,54,57,83,88
Ho! Ho! Ho! Who'd Be A Turkey
   At Christmas, 13,57,64,89
Holiday Inn, 9,35
Honey Roll, 9,34,57,63
Honky Cat, 10,18,35,40,44,54,58,
   63,74,75,77,78,83,85,88,90,92
Honky Tonk Woman, 33,77,78,
   84,87,89,91,92

Hourglass, 83
House Of Cards,14,65
Hymn 2000, 31

I Cry At Night, 20,67
Idol, 45,88
I Don't Care, 49
I Feel Like A Bullet (In The Gun
    Of Robert Ford), 15,19,
    41,54,65,88
If There's A God In Heaven
    (What's He Waiting For), 45
I Get A Little Bit Lonely, 81
I Heard It Through
    The Grapevine, 88
I Love You And That's All
    That Matters, 83
I Meant To Do My Work Today
    (A Day In The Country), 34
I'm Gonna Be A Teenage Idol, 38
Indian Sunset, 35,54,84,85,89,92
I Need You To Turn To, 32,53,
    84,89,91
Into The Old Man's Shoes, 9,57,89
I Saw Her Standing There, 14,24,
    65,80,83,88,93
Island Girl, 14,20,41,47,54,58,
    65,80,93
It Ain't Gonna Be Easy, 49
I Think I'm Gonna Kill Myself,
    37,88
It's Me That You Need, 8,10,54,
    57,62,89
I've Been Loving You, 8,83
I've Seen That Movie Too, 38,
    54,75,92
I've Seen The Saucers, 39,76

Jack Rabbit, 10,57,64,89
Jamaica Jerk Off, 38
Just A Little Bit, 8
Just Like Belgium, 59
Just Like Strange Rain, 8,57

King Must Die, The, 32

Lady Marmalade (John Lennon), 80
Lady Samantha, 8,10,18,52,
    57,62,88
Lady What's Tomorrow, 31
Levon, 35,53,63,74,90
Little Jeannie, 22,56,67
Love Lies Bleeding, 17,38,44,54,
    73,74,85,87,91
Lovesick, 20,66
Love So Cold, 24
Love Song, 33,44,54,84
Lucy In The Sky With Diamonds,
    13,19,24,47,54,58,65,77,78,80,
    83,88,90,93

Madman Across The Water,
    35,53,74
Madness, 52
Mama Can't Buy You Love,
    21,58,67
Meal Ticket (Gotta Get A), 41,53,
    80,86

Medley (Yell Help, Wednesday
    Night, Ugly), 41
Mellow, 37
Michelle's Song, 34
Midnight Creeper, 38,48,53
Mona Lisas & Mad Hatters 23,37,
    54,57,74,90
Mr Frantic, 8
My Baby Left Me (Live), 33,78,
    84,89,92
My Father's Gun, 32,84,89,92

Never Gonna Fall In Love
    Again, 56
Nobody Wins, 59
No Shoe Strings On Louise, 32

Oh My Love (John Lennon), 80
One Day At A Time, 13,65
One Horse Town, 45
Out Of The Blue, 45

Part-Time Love, 20,49,67
Philadelphia Freedom, 14,19,47,
    54,58,65,81
Pinball Wizard, 15,20,47,53,93
Pinky, 39,54,76

Razor Face, 35,63,84
Reminds Me Of You, 83
Return To Paradise, 49
Reverie, 52
Rock & Roll Madonna, 9,15,57,89
Rock Me When He's Gone, 83,84
Rocket Man (I Think It's Going
    To Be A Long Long Time), 9,16,
    18,37,40,44,48,54,57,58,63,
    74,75,76,78,83,88,90,92
Rotten Peaches, 35
Roy Rogers, 39
Rudolph The Red Nosed
    Reindeer, 75

Sails, 31
Salvation, 37
Sartorial Eloquence, 23,56
Saturday Night's Alright For
    Fighting, 10,16,20,39,40,53,64,
    73,75,88,92
Scaffold, The, 31
Screw You, 13,53,57,89
Seasons, 34
Shine On Through, 49
Shooting Star, 52
Shoulder Holster, 15,45,66
Sick City, 13,64
Since I Found You Baby, 8
Sing Me No Sad Songs, 83
Sitting Doing Nothing, 83
Sixty Years On 18,32,33,53,77,
    84,87,91
Skyline Pigeon, 10,18,31,44,48,
    52,57,63,84
Slave, 37,63
Slippin' & Slidin'
    (John Lennon), 80
Snookeroo, 90
Snow Queen, 15,16

Social Disease, 39
Solar Prestige A Gammon, 39,76
Someone Saved My Life Tonight,
    14,19,41,47,48,54,57,58,65,
    81,86,93
Someone's Final Song, 45
Song For Guy, 20,52,57,66
Son Of Your Father, 32
Sorry Seems To Be The Hardest
    Word, 15,45,47,57,58,66
Spotlight (John Lennon), 55
Stand By Me (John Lennon), 80
Steal Away Child, 23
Step Into Christmas, 13,64,89
Stinker, 39,76
Strangers, 21,67
Street Boogie, 55
Street Kids, 44,53
Sugar On The Floor, 14,65
Suzie (Dramas), 37,63,74,90
Sweet Painted Lady, 19,38,54

Tactics, 23
Take Me Back, 56
Take Me To The Pilot, 32,33,44,
    48,62,76,77,78,84,90
Talking Old Soldiers, 33
Tartan Coloured Lady, 83
Teacher I Need You, 38,48,53,74
Tell Me When The Whistle
    Blows, 41,86
Texan Love Song, 38,55
Theme From A Non-Existent
    TV Series, 45
This Is My Life (Bad Side Of
    The Moon), 78
Three Way Love Affair, 21,67
Thunder In The Night, 22,55
Ticking, 39,55,76
Tide Will Turn For Rebecca, The,
    83
Times Getting Tougher Than
    Tough, 8
Tiny Dancer, 35,54,57,63,74,84,90
Tonight, 45,88
Tower Of Babel, 41
Two Rooms At The End Of
    The World, 56

Val-Hala, 31
Victim Of Love, 21,55,67

Warm Love In A Cold World, 55
Warm Summer Rain, 62
We All Fall In Love Sometimes,
    17,41,55,86
Western Ford Gateway, 31
Whatever Gets You Through
    The Night, 24,79
Whenever You're Ready
    (We'll Go Steady Again), 10,16,
    53,57,64,89
When The First Tear Shows, 83
Where's The Shoorah, 45
Where To Now St Peter, 33,53
White Lady White Powder, 56
White Man Danger, 23,70
Whole Lotta Shakin', 85

Wide Eyed And Laughing, The, 45
Working Class Hero
    (John Lennon), 80
Writing, 41

Young Man's Blues (Screw You), 64
Your Sister Can't Twist
    (But She Can Rock & Roll), 39
Your Song, 9,16,18,32,40,54,57,
    58,62,73,74,75,77,78,84,85,87,
    90,91,92,93
You're So Static, 39,76,77,78,90
Your Starter For . . ., 45

A SHORT BIOGRAPHY

Elton John does not Speak for his Generation. Psychologists never analyse his appeal nor social historians ponder his relevance. His influence on musical trends has been minimal. Yet Elton John is one of the most famous men in the world, a singer who transcends rock, an "international celebrity" with all the trappings that this term implies. The days when he accounted for 2% of worldwide record sales are now over but his media presence remains unavoidable, even institutional.

Larger than life, Elton looms as the fantasy we must sometimes imagine for ourselves: the unexceptional transformed into the sensational. He was overweight, short-sighted and losing his hair yet he became the gaudiest, most extravagant, most exuberant rocker of his era, irrefutable proof that the meek shall indeed inherit the earth.

Proof, too, that rock, like all great art forms, is open to all.

Like the rocket man that inspired one of his best songs, Elton shot to fame in a spectacular thrust that outdistanced all his contemporaries. In purely statistical terms he was the most successful recording artist in the world during the four years that followed his 1971 breakthrough and at the same time he matured into an immensely entertaining, good natured and popular stage performer. His gradual decline, which was largely self-motivated, has left a gap which is unlikely to be filled in the current pop climate.

When low profiles were fashionable, Elton took the opposite tack. By his own volition he became a flashy superstar, revelling in his fame and wealth. His music combined mawkish sentimentality with some of the catchiest, most durable pop ever recorded. His taste and prolificacy offended purists but reached the impure and the support of this massive silent majority enabled Elton to realise his wildest dreams. In the end he bought his favourite football club.

The man who is Elton John was born Reginald Kenneth Dwight on March 25, 1947, at Pinner in Middlesex, a predominantly Conservative suburb less than a dozen miles north west of central London. He was the only child of Stanley and Sheila Dwight, a couple whose marriage was already failing. Though he'd once played trumpet alongside guitarist Bert Weedon in The Bob Miller Band, Stanley Dwight was a military careerist, a Squadron Leader with the RAF, and he was often away from home for long periods on tours of duty. He was out of the country when Reg was born and when he returned he showed no interest in his infant son. Later, when his spells at home became more frequent, he picked on his son incessantly.

"When I was a kid I was always being told not to do

things," Elton has said. "Until my parents got divorced I was suppressed and petrified by my father . . . I was never allowed to do this, that or the other.

"My father wasn't the slightest bit interested in me and he was a snob. I dreaded it when he came home."

A major source of conflict in the home was music, a strange contradiction since music seems to have been the only source of common interest in the Dwight household. Sheila Dwight was a keen record buyer, favouring show tunes and ballad singers, while Stanley was an avid fan of George Shearing. "I was brought up on my parents' pile of 78's," Elton recalls. "People like Guy Mitchell, Frankie Laine, Rosemary Clooney, Kay Starr, Billy May . . . all that early fifties stuff.

"My first favourite of all was Winifred Atwell . . . I was knocked out by her. Then my mother came home with two records, 'ABC Boogie' by Bill Haley and 'Heartbreak Hotel' by Elvis Presley. I'll never forget that: one was on Brunswick and the other on HMV. I really freaked when I heard them, and I went on from there. The first thing I ever read about Elvis was in a barber's shop, and I couldn't believe it."

Reg began playing piano by ear at the age of four. "I didn't have any formal training at first," he says. "I just sat down at the piano and could play." He liked to listen to a record and then rush over to the piano and play it from memory. "I used to listen to records all the time. I would buy records and file them. I could even tell you who published what, and I would stack them in a pile and look at the labels.

"I used to get a certain amount of pocket money each week, and I remember buying a Little Richard record, 'She's Got It' and 'The Girl Can't Help It', and my mother wouldn't let me play it. She liked rock but not Little Richard and I was really annoyed because it was my favourite record. I was really star struck and pop music was my whole life."

For a short period Reg took formal lessons on the piano but classical music was not to his liking. "He was being forced to play classics when he wanted to play popular tunes," says Sheila Dwight. "It wasn't until he was 11 or 12 that I found him a new teacher who let him play pop tunes, and from that time on this was all he was interested in."

Reg retreated into musical fantasy while the tension between his parents increased. He was keen on football and occasionally accompanied his father on excursions to watch Watford FC but he was forbidden to kick a ball in the garden lest he damage his father's precious rose trees. Neither was he allowed to wear stylish clothes. Musical aspirations were similarly crushed.

"My father didn't want me to go into music and I could never understand that because he'd been a

trumpeter in a band. I mean, he *did* influence me . . .
used to play me his George Shearing records. A four-
year-old listening to George Shearing is a bit off . . .
I was more into Guy Mitchell."

When Reg was ten Stanley and Sheila separated.
Soon they were divorced. His father remarried (and
produced four more children) but Reg continued to live
with the mother who had continually taken his side in
family quarrels. She cheerfully encouraged his musical
ambitions.

"I was terribly bitter about it at the time," said Elton
in 1975. "I see my dad now sometimes and I feel really
sorry that we didn't get closer. He has a new family that
he loves. I just wish that he could have loved me like
that too."

Reg had been attending Pinner County Grammar
School but at 11 he won a scholarship to The Royal
Academy of Music where he studied each Saturday
morning for the next five years. He had little aptitude
for academic subjects and, more often than not, played
truant, staying at home to play records or skipping off
to watch a game of football.

As a schoolboy Reg cut a chubby, ungainly figure
and when it was discovered he needed glasses he
naturally chose a pair with thick horn-rimmed frames in
emulation of yet another early hero, Buddy Holly.
Their owlish, slightly studious appearance only added
to his all round gracelessness but such matters failed to
hinder his musical ambition. He left school at 16, two
weeks before he was due to take an A-level exam in
music, and worked by day as a messenger for Mills
Music, a West End music publisher, for £4 a week. At
night he worked as a pianist, banging out standards in a
bar at the Northwood Hills Hotel in Pinner. "I used to
take my box around," he says. "People would put
donations in it. I was making a fortune compared to the
rest of the kids. I was getting about 35 quid a week."
This money went towards the electric piano and
amplifier that he would play in his first group The
Corvettes, who re-christened themselves Bluesology
after a tune by jazz guitarist Django Reinhardt.

"I was about 14 when I met a guy called Stuart
Brown who was the boy-friend of a friend of my
cousin's," Elton recalls. "I was extremely fat at the time
and when I told him I could play piano he just laughed.
He was a very moody sort of fellow and he played
guitar so I showed him and went through my Jerry Lee
Lewis bit. So we got this band together that played in
Boy Scout huts and we never had any amplifiers or
anything and that all faded away. It was just a pastime.

"Then a couple of years later I ran into him again
and he suggested we put another band together so we

did. That was Bluesology."

Reg and Stuart assembled a quartet from musicians who lived in the Harrow area. The first of many Bluesology line-ups comprised Mick Inkpen on drums, Rex Bishop on bass, Stuart on guitar and vocals, and Reg on an electric piano. Their initial repertoire centered on soul material industriously copied from the Stax and Tamla-Motown records that Reg had collected. "As a semi-pro group we got quite a bit of work, and we were ambitious and dedicated to the point of taking the plunge and adding a trumpet and a saxophone, which was partly because we wanted to expand our horizons and partly because of the emergence of Otis Redding style brass arrangements. Thinking we were a cut above the average club band, we concentrated on rather more obscure material, things like 'Times Are Getting Tougher Than Tough' by Jimmy Witherspoon.

"Our first sax player was unbelievable — used to travel down from St Albans for gigs but he decided to go off and play in the Queen Mary band, playing on Atlantic crossings, and so we got in Pat Hicks on trumpet and Dave Murphey on sax. They were much older than us, sort of frustrated jazz musicians, but as a result of the changes we were playing places like the Scotch of St James which was the discotheque."

Bluesology has achieved retrospective status as a semi-legendary club band of the Sixties but this is largely due to the subsequent career of their keyboard player. Despite attempts to attain success in their own right their main source of income came from backing visiting American soul singers. This work came through an association with agent Roy Tempest.

"One Saturday morning we did an audition at the Kilburn State and we aroused the interest of Roy Tempest who ran the agency which brought in the big American stars to tour," says Elton. "I simply couldn't dream of anything better. I was soul crazy at the time . . . used to spend all my money on soul records.

"Our first job was backing Wilson Pickett — can you imagine how we felt? He was such an important figure in the music we were playing, and here we were about to tour as his band. We went to rehearse with his guitarist but he didn't like our drummer, and he didn't particularly like the rest of us either, so that tour was blown out and we were very brought down. A little later we got offered the Major Lance tour, and to be sure of getting that we went out and bought every record he'd ever made. We learnt every song and rehearsed to the point where he arrived and was so impressed he didn't even feel the need to go through the songs making amendments."

Soon Bluesology was backing countless American stars — Billy Stewart, The Ink Spots, Patti Labelle and The Blue Bells (twice) and Doris Troy. The work was hard and Reg was forced to give up his job as a messenger. "We would hustle all over the place without any roadies," he said. "I don't know how much they got paid for these tours but one day during the Billy Stewart tour we played Douglas House, a US servicemen's club in London, at four in the afternoon, then rushed up to Birmingham to do both the Ritz and the Plaza ballrooms, and then back down to the Cue Club in London at four in the morning . . . and we had to load, unload and set up the equipment ourselves."

The average weekly pay was £15 a man and though the group cut three singles (two of which had Dwight compositions on their A-side), touring conditions remained frugal. Reg sang on the A-side of their first release — it was beyond the range of singer Stuart Brown — but his stage duty was limited to a malfunctioning Vox organ. His colleagues in Bluesology thought it unwise to feature a bespectacled, uncharismatic blimp as the group's front man.

After a while they left Tempest and joined Marquee Artists who found them work on the London R&B circuit (Scotch of St James, Cromwellian and Bag O'Nails Clubs) and at the Top Ten Club in Hamburg. Bassist Rex Bishop left the group to be replaced by Freddy Gandy, late of The Pink Fairies, and Mick Inkpen quit to be replaced by a drummer called Paul whose name has been forgotten in the sands of time. They went off on a tour of France and spent a month in a club in St Tropez. "The money was quite good and I was growing up . . . finding out what life was about," says Elton.

"When we came back to England, I started getting really frustrated and complex-ridden because I was extremely large, about 14 stone, and I was stuck behind a Vox Continental organ when what I really wanted to do was sing. There was no chance . . . we'd got into the rut of playing 'Knock On Wood' and 'Shake' every night for about four years."

Amongst their regular venues was The Cromwellian Club in London's Cromwell Road and it was here that Long John Baldry, the 6' 7" British blues singer, offered offered them a job as his full-time backing band. They accepted and for the next 12 months, their final year together, toured the UK playing rhythm and blues interpretations in the smooth, soft-edged style favoured by Baldry.

"Baldry's first move was to get Stuart to drop his guitar and concentrate entirely on vocals, to bring in another singer called Alan Walker and to turn it into a three singers up front type of band." Further reshuffles soon followed. "We got two new brass players, Mark Charig and Elton Dean, Neil Hubbard on guitar and Pete Gavin on drums and it wasn't a bad little band at that stage. A bit later, however, Alan Walker got the bullet and we auditioned potential girl singers because Baldry had decided it would be a good idea to get a bird out there in front too. He settled for Marsha Hunt. It worked out great. She looked good and got the blokes in the audience going but it was still down to the same old Wilson Pickett/Stax stuff."

In November of 1967 Baldry had a number one hit with a maudlin' ballad called "Let The Heartaches Begin" (which he'd recorded independently of Bluesology) and was henceforth attracted by the cabaret circuit. Within two weeks Stuart Brown and Marsha Hunt quit and the remaining members of Bluesology were obliged to provide back-up for Baldry's MOR aspirations. "We started playing big ballrooms," says Elton. "The high spot of our act was when Baldry used to sing his hit to a backing tape that we had to mime to.

"As Baldry's style changed towards the soft ballady stuff, we moved into cabaret and it was really beginning to bring me down. That Christmas we were doing three gigs a night for a while — the Sheffield Cavendish, Tito's in Stockton and South Shields Latino. We were the night club entertainment to help the food go down nicely. Well, that was it; I began looking through the papers to try to find a job. I didn't care what it was . . . working in a record shop, anything.

"I had to do something and I didn't want to join another band because quite honestly I wasn't that good an organist and I didn't look that good either. Really I wanted to be a singer but who would consider employing me in that capacity? Maybe Fred Bloggs & His Orchestra at Streatham Locarno or something of that sort . . . but nobody that I could enjoy working with. Although I didn't really want to write, I contined to toy with the idea because I thought that was the only way I'd get anywhere."

On June 17, 1967, Liberty Records placed an advertisement in New Musical Express seeking "musicians to form new group". The ad ran for several weeks and Reg was in Newcastle, on tour with Baldry, when he summoned up the courage to reply. A few days later he took two of his songs along to Ray Williams, the Liberty executive in charge of the auditions. "He said they were 'not bad' but I was a little disheartened because I thought they were knockout songs but I explained that I wasn't too good at lyrics and that I was looking for a lyric writer to form a team."

WATFORD

PROMOTED TO DIVISION II 1979

Reg was asked to attend an audition and when he arrived he was told to sing five songs. "I ended up singing five Jim Reeves' songs (among them 'He'll Have To Go' and 'I Love You Because') which I used to sing in the Northwood Hills Hotel. Well, of course, the audition was just dreadful . . . 'You must be joking,' they said, and I thought that my one golden chance of getting anywhere had gone down the drain.

"As I was leaving the studio, really brought down, this Ray Williams happened to mention that he'd had some lyrics from a guy called Bernie up in Lincolnshire somewhere and would I like to see them. I had a look and they didn't seem bad at all."

Among the lyrics that Williams gave him was a song called "Scarecrow" which Reg put to music. Williams was impressed and he introduced Reg to another music company with whom he was associated, Dick James Music. Over the coming weeks Elton made several demo recordings in DJM's 2-track studio, putting music to lyrics that arrived in the mail from Lincolnshire.

The engineer on these sessions was a guitarist called Caleb Quaye, an old acquaintance from Reg's days as a messenger at Mills Music. "He didn't recognise me because I'd lost a lot of weight during the previous months but when I told him he collapsed with laughter and we became the best of friends."

The songs that Reg wrote, the first ever Elton John/ Bernie Taupin compositions, were published through Ray Williams by Gralto Music, The Hollies' music publishing company. (Gralto was a pun on the names Graham, Alan and Tony). "All this time I was still in Bluesology," says Elton. "I was doing all these things behind their backs because I didn't want to give up a steady income until I'd sorted out an alternative. So between gigs I was up there making demos. It was just Caleb and me. Dick James didn't know what was going on at all.

"One day Ray Williams asked if I wanted to meet this guy who was sending all the lyrics in and I said 'Sure I do'. So in came Bernie Taupin, looking very green; it was only his second visit to London and he was staying with his aunt in Putney. I played him the songs, none of which he'd heard, and he was knocked out, so we decided to keep going as a team."

Bernie Taupin was born at Rasen in Lincolnshire on May 22, 1950. He was a fanciful character, a dreamer who took to writing scraps of poetry from an early age, imagining himself as a hero from Jack Kerouac's novels. He cultivated a gypsy image with long hair, a single earring and tattered clothes and had spent two years travelling around England doing casual work on farms and in factories.

"I spent a lot of time just doing nothing really," he said later. "I was out of work for long spells between various jobs. I was playing a lot of snooker and drinking a lot of beer, and staying out all night. Finally I got to a point where doing nothing just didn't appeal to me. I had to do something, something that I enjoyed."

He, too, had spotted the Liberty ad in New Musical Express though it was his mother who prodded him into replying. When Reg Dwight wrote asking for more lyrics Bernie churned them out at a frantic pace, submitting 50 songs for Reg to compose around. This early prolificacy would be maintained for eight years and became a hallmark of the partnership. When Reg and Bernie met at Ray Williams' behest, they became firm friends.

Reg's situation with Bluesology was brought to a head by Dick James, though it is doubtful whether he realised it at the time. It came to his attention that many aspiring writers were using his studio. "One day he discovered what was going on and had a purge," says Elton. " 'Who the hell are Reg Dwight and Bernie Taupin?' he shouted, and he got Caleb to play some of the stuff we'd recorded. I don't think he was very impressed but he agreed to sign us up because Caleb, who was his blue-eyed boy, said he thought it was good."

Very few successful music publishers have had the good fortune to discover gold on their doorstep more than once in a career but Dick James, a tubby, balding cigar-puffer in the Old Tin Pan Alley tradition, once a crooner with big bands, is one of them. In 1963, just after he started out in the publishing business, a humble Liverpudlian called Brian Epstein knocked on his door and the deal they struck made millions for Northern Songs and its parent company Dick James Music. James had no way of knowing then what The Beatles would become and neither, in 1968, did he realise the true potential of Reg Dwight and Bernie Taupin. Instead of encouraging them to follow their noses he offered them a three-year songwriting contract at £10 a week — less than Reg was getting with Bluesology but still sufficient incentive to quit the band — and encouraged them to write top twenty material, lightweight pop suitable for the Eurovision Song Contest or for recording by singers like Cilla Black, Engelbert Humperdinck and Tom Jones.

It was immediately after his final gig with Bluesology (on a plane flight from Scotland) that Reg, realising the limitations of his given name, decided on a change. "It was hopeless . . . it sounded like a library assistant," he says. "One of the guys in the group was Elton Dean, whose name I had always thought was real spiffy. I figured I could take part of his name but not all of it or he'd kick up. So I put it together with part of John Baldry's name and there it was . . . Elton John. Later I thought of changing it but nobody could come up with anything better." (With the addition of the nickname 'Hercules', this was later legalised by deed poll).

For almost two years the newly christened Elton and Bernie Taupin churned out lightweight material which they hoped would please Dick James. Bernie moved from Lincolnshire to stay at the Dwight home in Pinner for a while and then the pair rented a flat together at 29 Furlong Road, Islington. For six months Elton's girlfriend Linda stayed there too but the affair was not a happy one. "She hated my music," Elton admitted later. "She hated everything about me and I was completely dominated by her . . . it was like my father all over again. The thing that destroyed me was that she hated my music. Everything I'd write she'd put down." (When the relationship ended, Elton contemplated suicide, a period graphically described on the 1975 song "Someone Saved My Life Tonight").

Elton's depression was magnified by the working conditions at Dick James Music. They'd recorded a whole album's worth of songs which James rejected. "There were songs on it like 'Regimental Sergeant Zippo' and 'Watching The Planes Go By' but of all of the songs we wrote in that era, only a couple have ever seen the light of day. There's one called 'The Tide Will Turn For Rebecca', a Johnny Mathis type thing that Edward Woodward recorded, and one called 'I Can't Go On Living Without You' which Dick James put in for the Eurovision Song Contest. It got to the last six, the year that Lulu did the songs, and Cilla Black subsequently recorded it."

As a sideline Elton played piano on sessions for pop writers Roger Cook and Roger Greenaway who had a string of hits to their credit, notably those recorded by Blue Mink. "They said that the only way to make it was to work as we found best . . . they wrote to a formula that suited them, but they reckoned we should do what we wanted to do regardless of commercial considerations." This was sound advice but premature and it wasn't heeded when Philips signed Elton to a one-off singles deal in 1968. "I've Been Loving You", Elton's recording debut as a solo artist, was a gloomy and forgettable ballad more suited to an oily crooner.

Matters at DJM were not helped when Caleb Quaye had a blazing row with Dick James and left the company. "That meant there was nobody at DJM who was interested enough to help us," says Elton. "We went through a thoroughly depressing period until a guy called Steve Brown arrived as a plugger for the new

DJM label. He listened to our songs and though he liked them, he said there was nothing there that knocked him out . . . in other words they weren't very good. In fact he was right — they weren't very good but we didn't know that at the time and it really hurt us. He said that the fault lay in the fact that we were doing things half and half . . . partly as we wanted and partly as Dick wanted, and it was coming out as a mishmash. He told us to go and write what we really wanted to."

Further advice on similar lines came from a DJM publisher called Lionel Conway, who went on to head Island Records' publishing division, and the pair finally decided to ignore Dick James — the "Meal Ticket" they later wrote about — and write a batch of songs without commercial consideration. These songs, which included "Lady Samantha", comprised the material that made up Elton's first album "Empty Sky".

"I hated 'Lady Samantha' but Steve liked it and it came out and got a reasonable amount of airplay," Elton said later.

"I'd heard him playing some of his songs and I asked Dick James if I could produce 'Lady Samantha'," says Brown. "I hadn't any experience as a producer at all but I had been a musician. I played baritone sax for a time with Emile Ford and The Checkmates. So I went into Dick James' studio — it was a four-track studio and very primitive — and we spent an evening on 'Lady Samantha'.

"After the session we were all a bit despondent about it. We thought it probably shouldn't be released. But within the next ten days everybody started getting enthusiastic and it was released through Dick James' company on the Philips label. It got 120 airplays but didn't even make the top fifty."

"I'll always remember that session," says Elton. "We hired an electric piano which was so abysmally out of tune that I had to play round a lot of the notes. After it was finished I listened to it and thought it was awful . . . I told Steve that he ought to stick to plugging."

"Lady Samantha" was released in the second week of January, 1969, and though it never charted it went on to sell around 20,000 copies. It succeeded in getting Elton's name known within the music industry and was the deciding factor in Dick James' decision to allow Elton to record a whole album of the kind of songs he and Taupin felt comfortable writing. Such was Elton's pleasure at the prospect of making an album that he gave up working in the Musicland record shop in Soho, a part-time day job he'd taken to help make ends meet. During February and March of 1969 Elton recorded "Empty Sky" at Dick James' studio with Steve Brown producing the basic tracks and adding strings at Olympic.

Caleb Quaye assembled a studio band around Elton that included a drummer called Nigel Olsson (b. Wallasey, Cheshire, February 10, 1949) whose size belied his experience. Olsson had already drummed with Plastic Penny (on their hit single "Everything I Am"), The Spencer Davis Group (after Peter York quit) and the first aggregation of Uriah Heep. His closest musical ally was bass guitarist Dee Murray (b. Gillingham, Kent, April 3, 1946) with whom he'd played in the Davis group. Though Murray did not play on "Empty Sky", these two would soon become Elton's closest musical collaborators after Bernie Taupin.

"Making the 'Empty Sky' album still holds the nicest memories for me — because it was the first, I suppose," says Elton. "We used to walk back from the sessions at about four in the morning and stay at the Salvation Army headquarters in Oxford Street. Steve Brown's dad used to run the place, and he used to live above it. I used to sleep on the sofa. It's difficult to explain the amazing enthusiasm we felt as the album began to take shape, but I remember when we finished work on the title track . . . it just floored me. I thought it was the best thing I'd ever heard in my life."

Before the album was relased Elton signed with the DJM label and Dick James took over management responsibilities for both Elton and Bernie Taupin. In May Elton's first single on DJM "It's Me That You Need" was released — another flop — and the album followed in June. It was a folk based album, laced with harpsichord and flute, and though it sold only 2,000 copies on release, it drew attention to their latent ability as creators of catchy riffs and lyrical enigmas.

Elton and Bernie developed an unusual working method with Taupin delivering lyrics around which Elton would later compose. The words were never altered and Taupin had no way of knowing how his songs had been treated until Elton had finished writing the music. This passive communication, with zero interaction, would be maintained throughout their working relationship. "I really don't know what's going on in Bernie's mind," Elton said in 1972. "I ask him if a certain song is about a certain person or something like that, but I don't get any sense out of him."

Neither did the lyrics make much sense or even suggest a point of view. They were illusive, like word patterns, but they were easily memorable and this was the key to their success. Elton relied on the *sound* of words, not their literal meaning. His major talent, apart from an increasing ability to come up with catchy hook lines, was in the accent, pronunciation and phrasing of

Taupin's lyrics. In this way he made them *seem* significant, squeezed emotion from the nonsense, and made the words more memorable still.

Though as yet largely unknown to the public, the partnership was developing at a fast rate during 1969. Many songs were written but Steve Brown had decided to bow out of the picture as he felt unable to produce the orchestral arrangements that the songs warranted. George Martin, The Beatles' producer, was approached to produce Elton but he declined and in the end arranger Paul Buckmaster recommended his friend Gus Dudgeon. Both had recently been working with David Bowie and were responsible for the arrangement and production of Bowie's first hit "Space Oddity".

No thought was given to performing live at this point. Instead, the duo produced demos of new material — including "Your Song" — with which they hoped to interest producers. "Paul had a listen to a tape of 'Your Song' but, though he thought it was fantastic, he was worried that he wouldn't be able to do it justice. Eventually he agreed to work on them with us and he suggested that we go and see Gus," says Elton. "Gus played it cool at first . . . 'not bad,' he said as he was listening to our tapes, but eventually he agreed to do it."

Dick James agreed to spend £5,000 on Elton's second LP, a substantial sum at that time. The sessions were fixed for December and January, 1970, and in the meantime Elton sang on a number of sessions for other artists or on cover tracks that were released by Marble Arch and Music For Pleasure Records. At these sessions (recording songs like "My Baby Loves Loving", "United We Stand" and "Signed, Sealed, Delivered") he often sang alongside David Byron, later of Uriah Heep. Elton sang in a higher register while Byron took the lower keys.

"Elton John" was released in April, 1970. Though initial sales of 4,000 were disappointing, the album was praised by the critics for its rich texture, mood and emotion. With highly personal lyrics, lilting melodies and strong hooks, it set the pattern for almost everything that followed and was in no small way responsible for the upward momentum that Elton's career was shortly to take.

The stand-out track was "Your Song", an unashamedly romantic piece which went on to become one of Elton's most endearing classics. Two other songs, "Border Song" and "Take Me To The Pilot", were notable for their melodramatic delivery and curious lyrics, while the Buckmaster strings added an emotional quality which gave all the tracks a kind of maturity not often heard at this stage in an artist's career. There was an originality in the composition and arrangements that was both seductive and beguiling, an atmosphere of unforced grandeur that lent significance to the songs and melodies.

Many of the songs were covered by others. "A million groups did 'Pilot' and there were several versions of 'Sixty Years On' and 'Border Song', including a superb one by Aretha Franklin," says Elton. "Border Song" was chosen as the first single and Elton appeared for the first time on Top Of The Pops, a serious and studied young man whose glasses and demeanour put viewers in mind of an apprentice Randy Newman. This image was soon to change.

That summer Elton went back on the road for the first time since his days with Bluesology. At first he was reluctant — unhappy memories lingered — but Steve Brown persuaded him that the only way to promote the album was by performing live. Elton struck out as the leader of a trio with Olsson and Murray. He had hoped that Caleb Quaye would join them but Quaye elected instead to stay with Hookfoot, the group he had formed from other friends who worked the session circuit.

The first live performance by The Elton John Band was at the 1970 Pop Proms at London's Roundhouse on April 21, sharing a bill with headliners Tyrannosaurus Rex, The Pretty Things and Heavy Jelly. Other shows followed during the summer, some at colleges, some at clubs, some at recognised rock venues like London's Lyceum. Gradually his reputation spread.

Among the least appetising shows where Elton was booked to appear was a one-day outdoor event at the village of Crumlin near Halifax. The weather was atrocious and backstage squabbles broke out between groups over when (or perhaps even if) they should take the stage. That night, in the most appalling weather conditions, Elton came out of his shell. "Nigel suggested we try moving about on stage to keep warm," he says. "I realised that if I started jumping about, not caring what I'm doing, then at least I'd keep my ass warm."

So Elton did just that, leaping on to his piano, playing with his feet, even offering brandy to the first few rows of the shivering audience. He was the star of the event and the audience reaction was sufficient to convince Elton to inject a little frenzy into all his shows. Within 12 months it was to be his most notable characteristic.

At one point that summer there was a likelihood that Jeff Beck would join The Elton John Band. "Jeff came to talk to me after I'd done a set at The Speakeasy one

night . . . he said he'd really like to join the band," recalls Elton. "I obviously wasn't going to let an offer like this go by but at the same time I was worried that he might try to turn us into a wailing guitar group which I was always against. We set up rehearsals and I just simply couldn't believe how well Jeff fitted into the group. The crunch came when Jeff said, 'I don't really like your drummer too much — I'd like to bring Cozy (Powell) in'. We had a big meeting and I decided I'd rather keep just Nigel and Dee because we'd only been going for a short time and I was really enjoying it."

In September Elton flew to America for the first time to appear at The Troubadour Club in Los Angeles. Though his records had been released in the US (on the Congress and UNI labels), little had been achieved but Russ Regan, a UNI plugger, persuaded Dick James to invest $10,000 in a promotional visit that would include the Troubadour showcase. It was an extraordinary début.

Regan employed Norman Winter, a stunt-conscious publicist, to inject a little razzamatazz into the visit and Elton was met at the airport by a London style double-decker bus; hype it may have been, but at least people sat up and took notice.

"We'd flown to Los Angeles, 13 hours over the Pole in this jumbo jet, and we arrived to find this bloody great bus with 'Elton John has arrived' plastered on the side," says Elton. "It took us another two hours to get to the hotel."

Elton's expectations of the trip were low; his main pre-occupation was the opportunity to visit LA record shops. "I thought it was going to be a joke," he says. "I thought it was going to be a complete hype and disaster."

Such fears were unfounded and by the end of the first night he had worked the audience into a wild frenzy. Robert Hillburn, reviewing the show for the Los Angeles Times, wrote that "the first real superstar of the 70's has arrived" and Bill Graham, the rock promoter from San Francisco, called to offer Elton $5,000 for a show at either of his Fillmore auditoriums, the highest amount ever paid for a new act.

There followed a period of intense activity as the Elton John phenomenon just grew and grew. Elton developed a stage routine that became more and more frenzied. At a given point in the show he would kick over his piano stool, jump wildly at the keys and, if its lid was down, leap on top to rouse an audience; and then, after this exuberant display, he would switch styles completely and deliver a sentimental ballad in a tremulous style that bordered on pathos. Gradually he cast all inhibitions aside and his wardrobe became more and more colourful, star-spangled boots, jump-suits and hats. But most of all the impression he gave was of an artist enjoying himself in his work and communicating that enjoyment to his audience in what often seemed to be a spirit of cheerful self-mockery. Elton John-mania was on the boil: when Bob Dylan turned up to watch one of his American shows, Melody Maker plastered the banner headling "Dylan digs Elton" across its front page.

Elton's third album "Tumbleweed Connection" — recorded at Trident Studios at odd spells during the summer — was released in October. Less dependent on Paul Buckmaster's strings than "Elton John", it echoed Bernie Taupin's fascination with the American West and ranged in style from country blues to gospel. Its stand-out track "Country Comfort" was recorded by Rod Stewart, and "Burn Down The Mission", a frantic gospel shouter, now became Elton's closing number in concert. A lighter touch came with "Love Song" on which Elton duetted with Lesley Duncan.

"Your Song", released as a single in January of 1971, was an immediate hit and there appeared on the market a surfeit of Elton John records, not all of them up to the standard set by "Elton John" and "Tumbleweed Connection". "UNI Records released 'Tumbleweed' in the States while 'Elton John' was still in the top ten there and it went straight into the charts at number 25 with a bullet," says Elton. "Within a couple of weeks we had two albums in the top five and when we got back home all the press suddenly wanted to know us. Once we started getting all the publicity both those records zoomed up the charts in England too."

In April, however, the market was further swelled by two other albums, a film soundtrack ("Friends") and a live recording ("17.11.70"). The former was recorded in early 1970, well before success beckoned, and the latter was issued to combat bootlegs recorded from a live radio concert for WABC-FM in New York.

"We did the 'Friends' album in four weeks," says Elton. "Four weeks of very harrowing work. We did it at Olympic but for some reason got a terrible sound and had to do the whole lot again at Trident." He had made the album for film producer David Markham after Ritchie Havens turned the project down. It contained just five of his songs alongside film soundtrack material and was unrepresentative of the direction Elton's career was taking.

The live album, too, was substandard. "I agree that that album is not very good," Elton admitted later. "During our second tour of the States, which was mostly co-headlining with people like Leon Russell, The Byrds, Poco and The Kinks, we were asked if we'd like to do a live broadcast over the air. We didn't know it at the time but afterwards we found out that Steve Brown had arranged for an 8-track recording to be made and when we listened to it we thought it was quite good. We did a quick mix at DJM and I wanted it to come out because Dee and Nigel were featured very strongly.

"Looking back it's not a wonderful recording but I think it's valid despite the fact that saleswise it was a disaster. Even 'Empty Sky' has outsold that one in Britain, and in America it sold only 325,000 copies, compared with the previous two which did over a million. But it did mean that I had four albums in the US top thirty at the same time which hadn't been done since The Beatles."

Elton continued to tour relentlessly. During 1971 he toured England and America twice and also made trips to Australia and Japan. Neither did his recording schedule slow up to any degree. In November DJM released "Madman Across The Water", his sixth album in less than two years, an extraordinary work rate. (It took The Who over five years to release six albums and one of those was a collection of hit singles). Typically, after the praise he'd generated during the past 12 months, Elton now encountered criticism, especially in the UK.

"Madman" was only a minor disappointment — marking time instead of progressing — and in America it produced two hit singles "Levon" and "Tiny Dancer", the latter a tribute to Bernie Taupin's girlfriend Maxine, soon to become his wife and Elton's seamstress. "On reflection I like the songs (on 'Madman') but the vocals leave a lot to be desired," Elton said recently. It was to be the last time that Paul Buckmaster was brought in to enhance the string arrangements, and the guitarist on the sessions, Davey Johnstone (b. Edinburgh, May 6, 1951), late of folk band Magna Carta, was shortly to be invited to join Elton's road band.

Much of the material on "Madman" had been written while touring America and the sentiments expressed indicated that conditions on the road were far from comfortable. Nevertheless 1971 was an astonishing year for Elton. Cover stories, including one in Rolling Stone, appeared almost weekly and TV appearances, including an Andy Williams Show appearance with Ray Charles, a lifelong idol, were almost as frequent. The year ended with a long British tour that climaxed with a show at London's Royal Festival Hall where his trio was augmented by 35 musicians from the Royal Philharmonic Orchestra. Elton did not enjoy the experience.

"I thought the orchestra were cunts, every single one of them," he said the following year. "I just thought they gave a quarter of their best and they didn't take the event seriously. I felt so tense because I was uncomfortable playing with them. But it was all snide remarks during rehearsal. I sunk a lot of bread into it and I'll never do it again."

The following year opened with another bad experience. In January he was scheduled to appear at MIDEM, the music industry convention in Cannes where deal-makers gather for a week's indulgence amidst some of the most beautiful scenery in the world. At his showcase appearance Elton was due to follow Eric Burdon but Burdon overran and when Elton finally appeared his show was drowned out by Burdon's band War who continued playing behind the backdrop. Appearing again the following night Elton's show was again hi-jacked — by a curtain falling on his head.

Exhaustion was setting in. On the point of collapse, he took a forced break (postponing a planned UK tour in the process) during February and March, only to return to America for another long tour in April, May and June. "I was like a plate of jelly," Elton said. "My fingers were bleeding. I was overworked but we were so knocked out that people wanted us that we said yes to everything."

The danger of over-exposure was great but Elton overcame this by sheer amiability. After the American tour he retreated to a rented house in Malibu to recover from nervous exhaustion. In just over 18 months he'd risen from obscurity to a pinnacle of success, the back runner who confounded all odds.

Elton was still recuperating when he recorded "Honky Château" at Château D'Herouville, a studio in the French countryside not far from Paris, early in the New Year. This album marked a clear change of direction in Elton's music: it was the first he recorded with his road band as the basic studio unit and the first to back off from the introspective style, the hallmark of earlier records. Both the songs and their treatment were lighter, less refined, and the atmosphere was almost jolly, a welcome contrast to the sombre mood that dramatic string arrangements had brought to his first three hit albums.

"Honky Cat", one of the best riffs that Elton has ever written, shuffled along with toe-tapping gaiety; "Rocket Man", the international hit single, was a superior take-off of David Bowie's "Space Oddity"; "I Think I'm Going To Kill Myself" was exasperatingly light-hearted despite its melancholy title; and "Mona Lisas And Mad Hatters", the only introspective song on the album, was a touchingly evocative description of life in New York.

"Honky Château" also served to lay waste any lingering doubts about Elton's image. His concert style often seemed at odds with the material during 1971 but the new songs were ideal for the extrovert who emerged after these sessions. Now his concerts featured all the razzamatazz of Barnum & Bailey and gleefully mocked the laid-back pomposity of so many contemporaries. Elton now carried with him several wardrobes of exotic clothes, jump-suits trimmed with feathers, stack heeled silver boots and, by all accounts, £20,000 worth of personally customised spectacles, some of them illuminated, others large enough to mask his entire face. The clothes were often outrageously camp — his bisexuality would not become generally known until the late seventies — and his off-stage attire was no less gaudy.

The more outrageous he became, the more he was loved. In some peculiar way Elton managed to slice through age gaps with ease: there was no typical Elton John fan. He appealed to all ages, both sexes, all creeds and all income groups. He was neither threatening nor unwholesome; always he gave value for money and, like all who are committed, he genuinely *cared* about pop music, both his own and that of others.

Elton was a superior adjunct to that early seventies pigeon-hole, glitter rock. Scaling the ladder alongside him were David Bowie, as Ziggy Stardust, Marc Bolan, as the teenybop hero of T. Rex, and Rod Stewart, the flamboyant lead singer with The Faces. All these artists eschewed the instrumental virtuosity and serious demeanour that sprung up with the emergence of "progressive rock" in the late sixties and, instead, brought glamour back to popular music.

This was the kind of glamour reflected in the sleeve of "Don't Shoot Me I'm Only The Piano Player", a Hollywood poster pastiche with a ten page illustrated libretto, the kind of packaging that personified the Elton John of 1972/3. Inside Elton's eighth album was music as glossy as the outside, songs typified by "Daniel", a touching piece about a blind man who can find solace only in the hills of Spain. There were suggestions that this song was evidence of Elton's latent homosexuality (after all, he never *seemed* to have any girl friends) but this was laughed off in the casual bonhomie that Elton managed to exude in his many interviews.

"Crocodile Rock" and "Daniel" both became hit singles though the latter's release caused some controversy and suggested that kinks were appearing in Elton's business relationships. Dick James did not want "Daniel" to be released as a single. "We are releasing

'Daniel' as a single solely because of the pressure from Elton," said James. "It is also against the wishes of MCA who distribute Elton's records in America."

"It's one of the best songs we've ever written. I don't care if it's a hit or not . . . I just want it out," retorted Elton who promptly paid for all advertising from his own pocket on the understanding that he would be reimbursed if it reached the top ten.

Elton was proved right ("Daniel" made number 4 in England and number 2 in America) and from this point onwards he sought greater control over the way his career was handled. Already a new mananger was standing in the wings: John Reid, a small but quick-tempered Scotsman who had left his job at EMI Records to become Elton's personal manager. Together they planned the launch of Elton's own record company, Rocket Records, for 1973.

Rocket was planned not as a label for Elton's own records but as an outlet for artists in whom both took an interest — Davey Johnstone was an early signing — and whom Elton might produce at some time. Its arrival was heralded with much fanfare for at this stage Elton was at the peak of his career.

That year's American tour, lasting from August to October, broke house records hitherto held by Elvis and The Rolling Stones. He drew 28,000 to Arrow Head Stadium in Kansas City and his Hollywood Bowl concert was a spectacular of gargantuan dimensions involving lookalikes of Queen Elizabeth, the Pope, Groucho Marx, Elvis Presley, The Beatles, Batman and Robin and more. Elton followed them down a winding staircase as white doves were released into the California night. At one point in the show a live crocodile was brought on stage to dance to "Crocodile Rock".

Off stage Elton lived like an emperor. Unlike most of his fellow megastars (a term coined, incidentally, by Elton himself) he was unashamed of his vast wealth, determined to enjoy it in a way that somehow endeared him to fans and critics alike. He became known for his generosity, for giving away expensive presents, paintings, cars and jewellery, to close friends. His wildy extravagant life-style did not go unreported and he posed willingly for pictures outside his expensive properties or languishing amid interiors re-decorated in swish art-deco style, the epitome of suave good taste. His personal record collection was reputed to be among the largest in the world.

As his celebrity grew he was courted by (and photographed with) celebrities from every field of endeavour, professional athletes, actors and actresses, other musicians (Rod Stewart, a fellow scuffler from the sixties, remained a close friend), politicians and even royalty. He took tennis lessons from Billie-Jean King and appeared in the film of Pete Townshend's "Tommy" singing "Pinball Wizard" in stack heeled boots several feet above the ground. (Released against his wishes, "Pinball Wizard" became a hit single in 1976).

In October 1973 Elton released his most ambitious record to date, the sprawling "Yellow Brick Road", four sides of music that ranged from the Stones feel of "Saturday Night's Alright For Fighting", already a hit single, to the wistful "Candle In The Wind", a tribute to Marilyn Monroe. Elton had intended to record this album in Jamaica but his plans went awry after the studio was found to be unsuitable. All 18 tracks were written in three days at Dynamic Studio while his band sat around in the sun.

"We tried to put down 'Saturday Night' but it sounded terrible," Elton said later. "We spent three days in the studio attempting to get a decent sound but in the end we decided to quit and go back to the Château. Then overnight all our hired cars were driven away and we began to panic. Next they impounded all our equipment and wouldn't let us out of the hotel because the studio was supposed to pay our hotel expenses and it became quite frightening and there was most definitely a very dodgy feeling in Kingston towards us. If that wasn't enough there was a strike at Dynamic Sound so every time we drove in there were loads of pickets at the gate.

"We had a Volkswagen bus and they'd blow something like crushed fibreglass through the window at us which made us break out in a big rash. I've never been so glad to leave a place in my life."

The music on "Yellow Brick Road" transcended such problems. Two general themes inspired the songs: Hollywood mythology and doo-wop pop. One track "Bennie And The Jets", perhaps the catchiest hook that Elton has ever written, was an R&B hit in the States, a distinction of which Elton was immensely proud. Many other "Yellow Brick Road" songs became concert favourites: the instrumental "Funeral For A Friend" which segues into "Love Lies Bleeding"; the title track, an American chart topper in its own right; "Your Sister Can't Twist", a minor doo-wop masterpiece; and "Candle In The Wind", a shade mawkish but melodiously perfect all the same. The album stayed in the US top ten for nine months, his most commercially successful record ever.

"I don't like double albums as a rule," said Elton. "Ninety per cent of them are padded with long jams, eight minute cuts and the like. But 'Yellow Brick Road'

is like the ultimate Elton John album. It's got all my influences from the word go — it encompasses everything I ever wrote, everything I've ever sounded like."

There was, it seemed, an unquenchable thirst for Elton John records and Elton did not disappoint. Early in 1974 he cut his next album at Caribou, the Colorado mountain studio owned by Jim Guercio, producer and manager of Chicago. Unlike "Yellow Brick Road", "Caribou" was a down-to-earth album, marking time until another ambitious project could be realised. "It was recorded under the most excruciating of circumstances," said Elton. "We had eight days to do fourteen numbers . . . we did the backing tracks in two and a half days. It drove us crazy because there was a huge Japanese tour, then Australia and New Zealand, that could not be put off. And it was the first time we had recorded in America, and we just couldn't get adjusted to the monitoring system which was very flat. I never thought we'd get an album out of it."

Elton has since been critical of his vocal sound on "Caribou" but one of its strongest tracks "Don't Let The Sun Go Down On Me" (which he was reluctant to release) was later to be nominated for a Grammy Award for the best vocal performance of the year. Another "Caribou" song, "Solar Prestige A Gammon" gave rise to confusion for Taupin's lyrics were nothing more than a jumble of meaningless sounds: "Kool kar kyrie kay salmon/Hair ring molassis abounding/Common lap kitch/Sardin a poor floundin". It underlined the truism that Elton needed significant lyrics like a hole in the head.

The Tower Of Power brass section was brought in to beef up the arrangements on "Caribou". Percussionist Ray Cooper, who would soon join Elton's road band, was added to the rhythm section.

"Caribou" was released in June, 1974, and hot on its heels came "Greatest Hits Vol. 1", a gilt-edged compilation. Elton was no slouch on the singles front either: two "Caribou" cuts ("The Bitch Is Back" and "Don't Let The Sun") became hits that summer and in November he released a version of The Beatles "Lucy In The Sky With Diamonds". John Lennon played guitar and wrote the flipside "One Day At A Time".

Elton's friendship with Lennon was mutually fruitful. Earlier that year he'd played keyboards on the sessions that produced Lennon's "Whatever Gets You Through The Night" and, in a light moment, he made a bet with John that if the song reached number one in the US singles charts, John would appear on stage with Elton later in the year. Never imagining for one moment that this would happen, John agreed.

On November 28, 1974, the reclusive ex-Beatle kept his word, walking out onstage at New York's Madison Square Garden to perform three numbers ("Whatever Gets You Through The Night", "Lucy" and "I Saw Her Standing There") alongside Elton. The cheer that greeted Lennon brought tears to his eyes and the night will long be remembered, not least by Elton himself, as a highlight of his career.

(Elton subsequently became the godfather of Lennon and Yoko Ono's son Sean. When Lennon was assassinated in 1980 Elton was touring Australia and on the day of the silent tribute in New York's Central Park, Elton arranged a special church service at St Patrick's Cathedral, Melbourne, where he sang the 23rd psalm and read a lesson. His grief was heartfelt).

In 1975 Elton re-signed with MCA Records in America for a reported $8,000,000 advance. He was by this time unquestionably the hottest single act working in the record industry. By inviting the world not to take him too seriously he'd broadened his appeal to a scale that was quite unprecedented, and this universal celebrity coincided with a period when the record business was enjoying its most successful years since the invention of the phonograph.

"I couldn't believe the amount of money involved," said Elton later. "I'd never actually thought about having a lot of money and now I've earned an enormous amount but I've never become obsessed with it."

The first release of 1975 was "Philadelphia Freedom", a tribute to both disco producers Gamble and Huff and his friend Billie-Jean King, Philadelphians all. Coupled with a live version of "I Saw Her Standing There" from the Lennon concert, it crossed all barriers, topping both pop and R&B charts in the US.

In June Elton performed his biggest ever UK concert at Wembley Stadium, headlining a bill that included The Beach Boys, The Eagles and guitarist Joe Walsh. He took the opportunity to present almost all the material from his May album "Captain Fantastic And The Brown Dirt Cowboy", an error of judgement which resulted in The Beach Boys stealing the show.

The decision to confront such a large audience with so many unfamiliar songs was motivated by the importance Elton attached to his new work. "Captain Fantastic" was deeply autobiographical, thematic in concept, and for the first time in his career there was no confusion over the literal meaning of Bernie Taupin's lyrics. Many of them included acrid and scornful attacks on the business interests — publishers, agents, promoters and managers — who controlled his early career; not just the days of churning out pop material for Dick James but earlier times with Bluesology and playing for pennies at the Northwood Hills Hotel.

"It was entirely about us," said Elton. "The whole album was written from my end on the SS France going from Southampton to New York. I tried to get the music room but an opera singer had it booked the whole time except for when she scoffed her lunch for two hours. So every two hours at lunchtime I used to go in there and nip out to the piano and I wrote the whole of the 'Captain Fantastic' album."

Included in the lavish package was a generously illustrated libretto and a scrap book from the sixties with snapshots, clippings from Elton's 1969 diary and newspaper cuttings, all designed to add further weight to the album's historical significance.

"Captain Fantastic" was an immediate success — so immediate, in fact, that it became the first album ever to go straight to number one in the US Billboard charts in the week of release. "It was a pinnacle for me," said Elton. "That's as big as I got. It was a time when you couldn't switch a radio on in America without hearing one of my songs and people do get cheesed off. I was cheesed off with hearing myself as well and that's why I started, instead of just doing albums to try and do the occasional odd single."

There followed a gigantic American tour with a reshuffled band. Caleb Quaye joined Davey Johnstone on guitar, Roger Pope replaced Nigel Olsson on drums, American Kenny Passarelli replaced Dee Murray on bass, and James Newton Howard played an array of electronic keyboards to complement Elton's grand piano. Also on stage were back-up singers and percussionist Ray Cooper, an agile beanpole frantically thumping away on assorted conga drums and tom-toms.

The tour broke house records everywhere and for a show at the 55,000 seater Dodger Stadium in Los Angeles Elton magnanimously flew a planeload of friends, relations, Rocket employees and directors of Watford Football Club into California to watch the concert. He had become a director of the club earlier in the year and the responsibilities of this office would occupy more and more of his time as the Seventies wore on.

For the time being, however, there was no let up. Though "Captain Fantastic" and his "Greatest Hits" collection were still riding high in the charts, a second 1975 album "Rock Of The Westies" again recorded at Caribou, was released in October. In many respects "Westies" was similar to "Caribou", a return to basics in the wake of extravagance. Two hit singles, "Island Girl", a catchy, Jamaican influenced, toe-tapper, and "Grow Some Funk Of Your Own", a mediocre dance piece, highlighted the record.

The one distinction which had eluded Elton during these glory years was a chart-topping single in his home country. This he finally achieved in the summer of 1976 when a duet with Kiki Dee, "Don't Go Breaking My Heart", reached number one in the UK. Now, with this final triumph in his pocket, Elton decided to cut back. During concerts on his 1976 American tour he told audiences that "this will be the last tour in a long while".

"I feel like stopping for a time," he said. "I've done it for six years and I'm fed up with it. I'm not so much fed up with playing but I'm fed up with having no base and constantly roaming around. I just don't want the pressure of having to tour again for another two years or so.

"I guess I'll miss performing a little bit but over the last six years I've missed not having a home life. For the last two or three years I've just been like a wandering nomad. It's just so big that it's getting stupid and it's getting to be a bore . . . I just can't switch off. I used to like walking around New York but I can't do it any more. I can't get out of the hotel without some-body causing a fuss. I can't live my life in a shell like Elvis Presley."

That final tour, another swing through basketball arenas, included a record breaking six night stand at New York's Madison Square Garden. Earlier he had made a pilgrimage back to The Troubadour in Los Angeles to celebrate the fifth anniversay of his American début. Tickets sold at $250 each and all proceeds went to the Jules Stein Eye Institute, an appropriate charity in view of Elton's own sight problem.

Before long, however, his glasses — perhaps the most important trademark of all — would be replaced by contact lenses and his thinning hair replenished with a much publicised transplant. John Reid now managed Elton's affairs and the first of the two 1976 albums, "Here And There", a live recording of relatively old material, was his last record for DJM. Future albums appeared on his own Rocket label which was distributed in England through EMI.

The second album, the double "Blue Moves", was badly received by the press and, by Elton's own extraordinary standards, was a commercial failure. Wavering between self-doubt, self-pity and self-hatred, it was a doom laden excursion into uncharacteristic pretentiousness and it signalled a tapering off in popularity which Elton apparently welcomed.

Clearly he had decided th₄t enough was enough. In 1977 the decision was made to split with Bernie Taupin and other musical allies, make no live appearances in the immediate future and restrict recorded output to an album every 18 months, a productivity rate that bordered on stagnation by previous standards. Not until 1978 did a new album òf original material appear though a second "Greatest Hits" package, released in 1977, was a predictable million seller.

"When I came off the road I was very mentally tired, very unhappy," he said. "I had to decide if I could go on touring, and singing 'Yellow Brick Road' for the rest of my life which I hated and didn't want to do. I couldn't do anything for myself. I was a helpless young man and I became chairman of the football club which meant I had to hire people, fire people, go to the bank, do things that normal people do and people like me should be able to do. If I'd come off the road and had nothing to do, God knows what would have happened to me. But I had the football club to plunge into which I went in with full steam as if I was having a new band."

The football world was naturally sceptical when a pop star took over the chairmanship of a league club but Elton became truly dedicated to his new vocation, devoting much of his time and energy (and cash) to advancing their fortunes. To his enormous credit he confounded the sceptics and, under his chairmanship and Graham Taylor's management, Watford AFC rose auspiciously from League Division Four to League Division One in five seasons.

Despite Elton's pre-occupation with soccer, music was not entirely forgotten. He took part in a lighthearted studio romp with Jimmy Hill, Brian Moore and Eric Morecambe that produced "The Goaldigger Song" for the Goaldiggers' football charity in early 1977 and later in the year released a one-off single "Bite Your Lip (Get Up & Dance)" which somewhat ominously reached only as high as number 28 in the British charts. The high profile that Elton had enjoyed in the music press was not maintained though the national press, ever on the lookout for sensation, kept up their vigil with increased fervour.

When Elton admitted his bisexuality to Rolling Stone magazine, it was taken up with glee by Fleet Street. So, too, were reports that after playing in a football tournament, followed by a gruelling afternoon's tennis with Billie-Jean King, Elton collapsed and was rushed to hospital suffering from a heart attack. "It was just nervous exhaustion," he admitted later. "I went into hospital and it's great. If you want to sell more records just have a heart attack and go into hospital. It's incredible . . . I went in there and 'Part Time Love' was out and was doing 3,000 a day. As soon as I went into hospital it was doing 20,000."

"Part Time Love" was a track from Elton's 1978 album "A Single Man", his first without Bernie Taupin as lyricist. Producer Gus Dudgeon, too, had bowed out of the picture to be replaced by Elton's on-tour sound engineer Clive Franks. " 'Single Man' was an album that wasn't meant to be an album," said Elton later. "I went into the studio and did a record of 'Ego' which was a two-year-old song Bernie and I had written, and also a song called 'Shine On Through' which Gary Osborne and I had written. And because I hadn't written for so long I got writer's diarrhoea as I call it and suddenly I began to write melodies first. Gary was around and I had a few ideas for a certain line to the songs, and certain titles, and we had great fun doing it."

Among the other tracks recorded for "A Single Man" was "Song For Guy", Elton's first instrumental hit which was titled as a tribute to Guy Burchett, the Rocket Records delivery boy who was killed in a motor cycle accident around the time it was written. It reached number 4 in the UK charts — Elton's biggest hit of the late seventies.

DJM Records, meanwhile, busied themselves with an extensive programme of re-releases; early hit singles were released back to back and material from albums was re-packaged in a series of records designed to spotlight individual aspects of Elton's prolific output. A K-Tel collection — largely redundant because of the earlier "Greatest Hits" albums — was nevertheless a big seller after a TV marketing campaign.

Elton chose to experiment with a variety of different writers and producers during 1978, among them Thom Bell, the Philadelphia based producer of The Stylistics and Detroit Spinners. "I was delighted with the rhythm tracks . . . there was one song Bernie and I wrote, and one song that Gary and I wrote and there were four of Thom Bell's own songs. Then I heard the mixes and I decided to shelve them for a year because it was too saccharine. Eventually I put it out as a maxi-single in England.

"It was an indulgence on my part wanting to work with somebody for a new experience but Thom Bell taught me a lot . . . he taught me how to use my voice in a lower register."

In 1979 Elton elected to go back on the road with Ray Cooper as his sole accompanist. He played over 100 concerts in America and Europe and performed memorable concerts in Moscow and Leningrad. "I wanted to go out with just myself and then Ray and prove that I could do it on my own, to play soft numbers, to play rock and roll and to go to places that I'd never been before.

"We wrote a letter, an official letter, to the Russian people and we had a reply back in eight days, a very polite one saying, 'We'd love to have you.' They came over to see our show in Oxford." The Russian experience, which was filmed and later shown on television, was a moving experience for Elton. "I remember crying my eyes out on a train going from Leningrad to Moscow because all these kids, hundreds of fans who followed us around everywhere, were throwing all their favourite things in the window . . . . the friendliest, warmest people. We spent ten days there and I had the most fantastic time, culturally as well, seeing the most beautiful things."

In London Elton and Ray played the Drury Lane Theatre and backstage he became re-acquainted with an old friend, the noted disco producer Pete Bellotte. Bellotte suggested that Elton might make a disco album. "I said sure," recalls Elton. "I said I'd do it providing he got others to write the songs and play the backing tracks. Then later I went to Germany and put the vocals on top."

The result was "Victim Of Love", his much criticised 1979 album. "It didn't do my career a lot of good but I don't regret doing it whatsoever . . . I can understand why it wasn't successful. I enjoyed it, it was self-indulgent, but in the next few years people will have to expect more self-indulgent things·from me to appear."

Inspired by the success of his tour with Ray Cooper Elton went back on the road in 1980 and performed over 40 dates in the US, including an open air concert in New York's Central Park before an audience estimated at more than 400,000. He re-assembled his original group for the trip (Johnstone, Murray and Olsson) and added James Newton-Howard, Richie Zito and Tim Renwick to the line-up. The same band toured Britain in 1982 and Elton earned the nickname of 'Lord Choc Ice' for the bizarre Ruritanian officer's outfit that he wore.

After the lull of the previous three years Elton also stepped up his recorded output. In 1980, at the age of 33, Elton released his 21st album, "21 At 33". The songs were a mixture of collaborations with Bernie Taupin, Gary Osborne, Tom Robinson and Judy Tzuke. "I'd always encouraged Bernie to write with other people . . . there was never any feud between us . . . it's the typical thing that you read in the papers just because he lived in America and I had an album out and he had an album out with different people, the tongues started to wag."

By the eighties Elton's record sales were beginning

to level off and hit singles became thin on the ground. For "The Fox" (1981) he switched to the Geffen label in America and the albums "Jump Up" (1982) and "Too Low For Zero" (1983) were recorded on the Caribbean island of Montserrat. Tickets for his concerts, as always, were hard to come by but the mania that surrounded his presence in the early seventies, the mechanical regularity with which he ascended the charts, was no longer in evidence. It's more than possible he prefers it that way. His 1983 hit single "I'm Still Standing" was appropriately titled.

It was inevitable that Elton found himself unable to maintain the creative and commercial pace at which his career once travelled. Unlike many British rock stars in his income bracket he has elected to remain in England, at an impressive mansion near Old Windsor, instead of relocating to an overseas tax haven. He no longer courts publicity and seems to prefer the company of the football world to the current music scene. Billy Joel, the American pianist/songwriter who shamelessly aped Elton's style at the outset of his own career, now sells more records than his mentor but he is unlikely ever to eclipse Elton's accomplishments in overall sales.

Neither, for that matter, is anyone likely to eclipse the extraordinary saturation level that Elton enjoyed between 1972 and 1976. Pop is different now: fewer records are sold by more artists and the day of the megastar is over. This, in the long term, is not such a bad thing but Elton Hercules John, in his heyday, carried the title with dignity, good grace and a refreshing sense of uncharacteristic humility.

Chris Charlesworth 1983

(This essay included quotes taken from interviews with Elton John by myself, John Tobler, Andy Peebles, Greg Shaw, Caroline Coon, Roy Carr and Charles Shaar Murray, Richard Williams and Chris Welch).

UPDATE 1981-83

65 **LOVING YOU IS SWEETER THAN EVER***
Stevie Wonder/Ivy Hunter
24 HOURS** *Kiki Dee/Gary Osborne/Reid Kaelin*
Ariola ARO 269. Released November 1981
*Duet with Kiki Dee.
**Kiki Dee track.
Producer: Pip Williams

66 **BLUE EYES** *John/Osborne*
HEY PAPA LEGBA *John/Taupin*
Rocket XPRES 71. Released March 12, 1982
Producer: Chris Thomas (A)
Elton John and Clive Franks (B)

67 **EMPTY GARDEN** *John/Taupin*
TAKE ME DOWN TO THE OCEAN *John/Osborne*
Rocket XPRES 77. (Also 7-inch picture disc,
Rocket XPPIC 77). Released May 28, 1982
Producer: Chris Thomas (A)
Elton John and Clive Franks (B)

68 **PRINCESS** *John/Osborne*
THE RETREAT *John/Taupin*
Rocket XPRES 85. Released September 1982
Producer: Chris Thomas (A)
Elton John and Clive Franks (B)

69 **ALL QUIET ON THE WESTERN FRONT** *John/Taupin*
WHERE HAVE ALL THE GOOD TIMES GONE
John/Taupin
Rocket XPRES 88. Released November 12, 1982
Producer: Chris Thomas (A&B)

70 **I GUESS THAT'S WHY THEY CALL IT THE BLUES**
John/Taupin/Johnstone
LORD CHOC ICE GOES MENTAL
Rocket XPRES 91. Released April 1983
Producer: Chris Thomas (A)

71 **I'M STILL STANDING** *John/Taupin*
EARN WHILE YOU LEARN
Rocket EJS 1. Released July 1983
(Also 12-inch Rocket EJS 112 & 7-inch picture
disc Rocket EJPIC 1)
Producer: Chris Thomas (A)

72 **KISS THE BRIDE** *John/Taupin*
DREAMBOAT
Rocket EJS 2. Released October 1983
(Also 12-inch Rocket EJS 212)
Producer: Chris Thomas (A)

73 **KISS THE BRIDE*** *John/Taupin*
DREAMBOAT**
EGO*** *John/Taupin*
SONG FOR GUY*** *John*
Rocket 7-inch double single EJS 222.
Released October 1983
Producer: *Chris Thomas, ***Elton John and Clive
Franks

74 **COLD AS CHRISTMAS** *John/Taupin*
CRYSTAL *John/Taupin*
Rocket EJS 3. Released November 1983
Producer: Chris Thomas

75 **COLD AS CHRISTMAS*** *John/Taupin*
CRYSTAL* *John/Taupin*
DON'T GO BREAKING MY HEART** *Orson/Blanche*
SNOW QUEEN** *John/Taupin/Dee/Johnstone/Nutter*
Rocket EJS 33. Released December 1983
Producer: *Chris Thomas, **Gus Dudgeon

THE ALBUM
Hallmark SHM 3088 (UK)
Released September 1981 (UK)
Producer: Gus Dudgeon
Studios: Various
Recorded: Various
All compositions by Elton John and Bernie Taupin.
Side One:
1. Goodbye Yellow Brick Road
2. Burn Down The Mission
3. Sixty Years On
4. Crocodile Rock
5. Lucy In The Sky With Diamonds
6. Rock And Roll Madonna
Side Two:
1. Country Comfort
2. Harmony
3. Sweet Painted Lady
4. Pinball Wizard
5. Skyline Pigeon
6. Lady Samantha

JUMP UP
Rocket HISPD 127 (UK): Geffen GHS 2013 (US).
Released April 9 1982 (UK): April 1982 (US).
Producer: Chris Thomas
Studios:
Recorded:
All compositions by Elton John/Bernie Taupin
unless otherwise stated.
Side One:
1. Dear John *Elton John/Gary Osborne*
2. Spiteful Child
3. Ball And Chain *Elton John/Gary Osborne*
4. Legal Boys *Elton John/Tim Rice*
5. I Am Your Robot
6. Blue Eyes *Elton John/Gary Osborne*
Side Two:
1. Empty Garden

2. Princess *Elton John/Gary Osborne*
3. Where Have All The Good·Times Gone
4. All Quiet On The Western Front

LOVE SONGS
TV TVA3 (UK)
Released November, 1982 (UK)
Producers: Elton John & Clive Franks except * by
Chris Thomas and ** by Gus Dudgeon.
Studios: Various
Recorded:
Side One:
1. Blue Eyes* *(John/Osborne)*
2. Little Jeannie *(John/Osborne)*
3. Sartorial Eloquence *(John/Robinson)*
4. Shine On Through *(John/Osborne)*
5. Chloe *(John/Osborne)*
6. Elton's Song *(John/Robinson)*
7. Tonight** *(John/Taupin)*
8. Song For Guy *(John)*
Side Two:
1. Sorry Seems To Be The Hardest Word** *(John/Taupin)*
2. Princess* *(John/Osborne)*
3. Chameleon** *(John/Taupin)*
4. Return To Paradise *(John/Osborne)*
5. Never Gonna Fall In Love Again *(John/Robinson)*
6. Strangers *(John/Osborne)*
7. Someone's Final Song** *(John/Taupin)*
8. All Quiet On The Western Front *(John/Taupin)*

TOO LOW FOR ZERO
Rocket HISPD 24 (UK); Geffen GHS 4006 (US).
Released June 1983 (UK); May 23 1983 (US)
Producer: Chris Thomas
Studio: Air Studios, Montserrat; Sunset Sound,
Hollywood, USA.
Recorded:
Side One:
1. Cold As Christmas *(John/Taupin)*

2. I'm Still Standing *(John/Taupin)*
3. Too Low For Zero *(John/Taupin)*
4. Religion *(John/Taupin)*
5. I Guess That's Why They Call It The Blues
(John/Taupin/Johnstone)
Side Two:
1. Crystal *(John/Taupin)*
2. Kiss The Bride *(John/Taupin)*
3. Whipping Boy *(John/Taupin)*
4. My Baby's A Saint *(John/Taupin)*
5. One More Arrow *(John/Taupin)*
Musicians: Elton John; Davey Johnstone; Dee Murray;
Nigel Olsson; James Newton Howard (string
arrangement on 'One More Arrow'); Ray Cooper
(percussion on 'Cold As Christmas'); Skaila Kanga (harp
on 'Cold As Christmas'); Stevie Wonder (harmonica on
'I Guess That's Why They Call It The Blues').

THE NEW COLLECTION
Everest CBR 1027 (UK)
Released   1983 (UK)
Producer: Gus Dudgeon
Studios: Various
All compositions by Elton John and Bernie Taupin
except * by John Lennon and ** by John Lennon
and Paul McCartney.
Side One:
1. Crocodile Rock
2. Don't Let The Sun Go Down On Me
3. Saturday Night's Alright (For Fighting)
4. It's Me That You Need
5. Someone Saved My Life Tonight
6. Whatever Gets You Through The Night*
7. Lucy In The Sky With Diamonds**
Side Two:
1. The Bitch Is Back
2. High Flying Bird
3. Elderberry Wine
4. Candle In The Wind
5. Your Sister Can't Twist (But She Can Rock And Roll)
6. Daniel

37 **NOBODY WINS** *John/Osborne*
FOOLS IN FASHIONS *John/Taupin*
Geffen GFS 49722. Released April 1981
Producer: Chris Thomas (A), Elton John
& Clive Franks (B)

38 **CHLOE** *Elton John/Gary Osborne*
Geffen GFS 49788. Released July 1981
Producer: Chris Thomas (A)

39 **EMPTY GARDEN** *John/Taupin*
TAKE ME DOWN TO THE OCEAN *John/Osborne*
Geffen GEF 50049. Released March 1982
Producer: Chris Thomas (A), Elton John &
Clive Franks (B)

40 **BLUE EYES** *John/Osborne*
HEY PAPA LEGBA *John/Taupin*
Geffen 7-29954. Released July 1982
Producer: Chris Thomas (A), Elton John &
Clive Franks (B)

41 **I'M STILL STANDING** *John/Taupin*
EARN WHILE YOU LEARN
Geffen 7-29639. Released April 1983
Producer: Chris Thomas (A)

42 **KISS THE BRIDE** *John/Taupin*
DREAMBOAT
Geffen 7-29568. Released July 1983.
Producer: Chris Thomas (A)

43 **I GUESS THAT'S WHY THEY CALL IT THE BLUES**
John/Taupin/Johnstone
LORD CHOC ICE GOES MENTAL
Geffen 7-29460. Released October 1983.
Producer: Chris Thomas (A)